WHAT IS "CHURCH?"

CHURCH
at the
CROSSROAD

Preston McNutt

DEDICATION

This book is lovingly dedicated to Sherra DeLynne Melton McNutt, my wife and best friend for nearly four decades. From the beginning, she made our house a home and our home a castle. *She believed in me!* As you'll see in Chapter Five, it was supreme confidence Jesus expressed toward His disciples that inspired them to *turn the world upside down for Christ*[1] and ultimately to give their lives for the sake of His message. *He believed in them!*

DeLynne graduated from this earthly life February 18, 2014. She wore the cloak of the sweet character of her Savior better than anyone I've ever known before or since. She loved deeply and without regard for anything in return. Her influence is evident in every life she touched, and those lives were many. The deep pain of her loss together with the deep joy of the hope of Resurrection are perfectly expressed in this quote found on a gravestone in a cemetery in Ireland:

'Death leaves a heartache no one can heal; love leaves a memory no ~~one~~ can steal.'

---

[1] **Act 17:6** And when they found them not, they drew Jason and certain brethren unto the rulers of the city, crying, These that have turned the world upside down are come hither also;

CONTENTS

PROLOGUE

Perusing today's news headlines is a bit like flipping through a Rolodex on speed dial. Our senses are assaulted daily with a dizzying dose of attention grabbing, gut wrenching, titillating, often times horrifying headlines so fast one can hardly take it all in.

One disappointing but all too common human trait is that our first instinct when thrust onto the horns of a dilemma is not to search for the truth but to take sides and to make assumptions. The tendency is for people to line up on one side or the other, and once entrenched, to set about finding facts that support what they already believe.

Events in the U.S. in 2015 stand as a stark reminder of this phenomenon with social effects that will be felt for decades. The tragic events surrounding the deaths of Michael Brown, Eric Garner and Freddie Gray, along with a growing list of randomly targeted police officers, clearly reveal this common trait in humanity. People defending African American victims sought to explain away or ignore the evidence that suggested there was anything other than police brutality. Those defending the actions of the officers responsible for those deaths insist violence was warranted regardless of a growing body of bothersome video evidence clearly showing an increasingly militarized police force.

In the Fall of that year, the Supreme Court of the United States handed down its decision on their interpretation of the equality clause. And while the world was distracted with the unrestrained display of zeal in the global LGBT community, the U.S. Congress went right on passing laws designed to eviscerate the Constitution.

In each of these cases, rather than seek solutions to the problems that are at the root of much social unrest, people cherry-pick snippets of information that fit their worldview. Truth is always the first casualty when this happens. Race baiters who want to say that cops hate all African Americans will interpret the data that way. People who say that the use of force by police is always justified will interpret the data that way. People who say homosexuality is a constitutionally protected *right* will interpret the data that way. The reason for this, in my opinion, is that most people have already decided where they land on the issue, and they frame the information to support the conclusions they have already drawn.

A popular refrain introduced into American vernacular recently is *"black lives matter."* I agree. **All** lives matter. So does the truth. Truth matters. In the chilling words of George Orwell *"In an age of universal deceit, telling the truth becomes a revolutionary act."* We have become the world that he warned us about. This tendency in humans to read their own presuppositions or biases into and onto the text is called *eisegesis* in linguistic parlance.

↳ *PRONOUNCED ?*

The purpose of this book is two-fold. **Number one**: to challenge Christians to do a spiritual inventory, something I believe we should do regularly as believers. We're told to examine ourselves[2], to see if we are truly walking in the faith. Sometimes that requires a brutally honest self-appraisal of exactly what we believe and why we believe it. Are our beliefs truly Scriptural or is our faith based on the interpretations of others that we've simply accepted as truth? **Number two**: the author wants to say in clear unvarnished terms what he believes and teaches and why. They are not new teachings or beliefs of this writer. For those who mistakenly see these as new beliefs not adhered to in the past, maybe it's time to stand up and unequivocally declare what I have believed for many years but in a misguided concern for other people's feelings failed to clearly articulate in some circles. That was wrong and I fully repent of that failure. That said, the rock solid foundation of my faith is this: ***By grace are we saved through faith and that not of ourselves. It is the gift of God, not of works lest any man should boast. For we are his workmanship, created in Christ Jesus unto good works, which God hath before ordained that we should walk in them.*** - Eph. 2:8-10

~~The Church of Jesus Christ is at~~ a crossroad, a crisis of identity. Judgment

[2] **2Co 13:5** Examine yourselves, whether ye be in the faith; prove your own selves …

begins in the House of God. The earth is rumbling with clear signs of end time birth pains. We the Church, built upon the foundation of God's Word, find ourselves in the valley of decision. Will we stand boldly proclaiming to the world and to the enemy of mankind the **whole counsel of God**, or will we maintain the status quo, presenting a fractured Word stripped of its Jewish roots, while the Adversary robs us of our rightful unity of the Body and inseparable unity of the Scriptures? I hope to show by the end of this book evidence of the persistent dismantling of God's Word by the Adversary from the very beginning and show why we, the Body of Christ, the Church, are at a critical juncture, why we are the **<u>Church at the Crossroad.</u>**

WHAT'S HIS GOAL HERE w/ THIS TEAM?

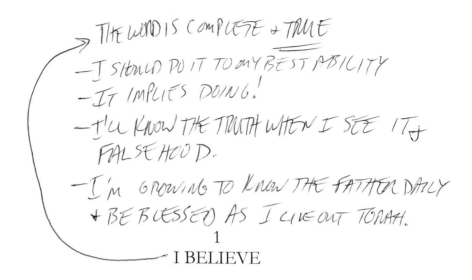

THE WORD IS COMPLETE & TRUE

— I SHOULD DO IT TO MY BEST ABILITY

— IT IMPLIES DOING!

— I'LL KNOW THE TRUTH WHEN I SEE IT & FALSEHOOD.

— I'M GROWING TO KNOW THE FATHER DAILY + BE BLESSED AS I LIVE OUT TORAH.

1
I BELIEVE

I believe. These words are the cornerstone of Christian faith. Belief in and of itself is powerless, even dangerous in some cases. I may believe I can fly under my own power, but flying off the edge of a tall building is sure to lead to a dissatisfying and sudden change in my world view.

As one person said, I'm not afraid of heights. I'm not even afraid of falling from a great height. It's the sudden stop that gives me great concern.

It is not enough to just believe. It is critical that the object of our belief be grounded in reality. For this reason, to be Christian means to believe *'For God so loved the world that he gave his only begotten Son, that whosoever believeth in him should not perish, but have everlasting life.'*[3]

This and many other Bible verses point to faith in Jesus Christ as the foundational confession that brings a person, a sinner, into the redemptive grace of a loving God.

Pontius Pilate, the Governor of Judea during the time Jesus walked the earth, asked a universally pertinent question that resonates in the heart of every human: *what is truth?* Is truth a philosophical concept? Is it a matter of subjective reality, whatever one perceives as truth is truth to that person? Is truth found in a mathematical formula, a set of precepts that define reality and once grasped place a person on a plane of higher knowledge?

---

[3] Jn. 3:16

TRUTH?

1

Just the Facts Ma'am

Many will remember Sgt. Joe Friday from the 1950's radio and later television series <u>Dragnet</u> and his signature phrase. Week after week, he and his partner solved every crime that was put on their desk with dogged persistence and tenacious pursuit of the facts of a case.

We humans tend to cling to selected facts as a way to justify our beliefs about how the world works. We add facts to our personal store of knowledge that agrees with what we already know. Not that that is a bad thing in and of itself. But confirmation bias can lock a person into a certain belief, unwilling or unable to assimilate new facts that may seem to contradict one's current worldview.

[handwritten note: CATHOLIC & SUCH]

Facts are funny things. Would you jump out of an airplane without a parachute for a million dollars? The answer is likely going to be no.

The plane is sitting on the tarmac. Aha! You might be a million dollars richer if only you had known that additional fact!

Niels Bohr, the Danish physicist who won the Nobel Prize for his work on atom structures, said this:

"The opposite of a fact is falsehood, but the opposite of one profound truth may very well be another profound truth."

[handwritten note: STUDY IS VITAL TO LEARNING TRUTH]

Two essential Bible doctrines that underscore this phenomenon are the principles of freedom of choice - free will – and the concept of predestination, of believers having been chosen before the foundation of the world. Both are Biblical, both are true, yet they seem to stand in direct contradiction to one another.

If God chooses who is to be saved before the individual is even born, how can that person's will be free to accept or reject the offer of salvation? If one is foreordained to salvation, then isn't it a foregone conclusion that the person will be saved irrespective of his or her own volition? Yet the Bible is clear that one must receive salvation as an act of the will, a personal choice based on faith. One is free to accept or reject God's offer of salvation, putting the responsibility squarely on the shoulders of the individual to make the choice.

2

Both doctrines are factual. Both are true. And both stand in stark contrast to one another, seeming to break all laws of logic.

It is true that one plus one equals two. It is true that E=MC². It is also true that facts may be true, but are facts truth? *ARE FACTS TRUTH?*

The problem with facts being the determining factor in deciding truth is that oftentimes facts have a tendency to skew the truth in favor of the viewer's perspective. Ten people may see an accident and all ten present the facts of the event and all ten may have differing views of what actually occurred. The resulting conclusion of what actually happened is skewed by facts that differ based on individual perceptions. The person viewing the accident from a third story window may have facts that are not available or visible to the person viewing it from ground level.

For someone with a predisposition to establish or further a particular paradigm, changing or manipulating the facts to fit the narrative is a powerful tool in accomplishing the goal. While the facts may be true, the conclusion drawn from biased handling of facts may lead to a supposition that is far from the truth of the matter.

Dr. Neil deGrasse Tyson, a popular physics expositor and television personality, was dismissed from jury duty, not once but twice, because of his propensity for letting factual evidence speak for itself without biased testimony. Here's the full quote; emphasis is mine:

"In 2002, having spent more than three years in one residence for the first time in my life, I got called for jury duty. I show up on time, ready to serve. When we get to the voir dire, the lawyer says to me, 'I see you're an astrophysicist. What's that?' I answer, 'Astrophysics is the laws of physics, applied to the universe—the Big Bang, black holes, that sort of thing.' Then he asks, 'What do you teach at Princeton?' and I say, 'I teach a class on the evaluation of evidence and the **relative unreliability of eyewitness testimony.'** *Five minutes later, I'm on the street.*

A few years later, jury duty again. The judge states that the defendant is charged with possession of 1,700 milligrams of cocaine. It was found on his body, he was arrested, and he is now on trial. This time, after the Q&A is over, the judge asks us whether there are any questions we'd like to ask the court, and I say, 'yes, Your Honor. Why did you say he was in possession of 1,700 milligrams of cocaine? That equals 1.7 grams. The 'thousand' cancels with the 'milli-' and you get 1.7 grams, which is less than the weight of a dime.' *Again I'm out on the street."* — *Neil deGrasse Tyson, Space Chronicles: Facing the Ultimate Frontier.*

Do you see how phrasing the charge with the words 1700 milligrams can trigger an emotional response to a seemingly huge amount of cocaine, irrespective of the fact that the amount was miniscule in reality? So it is with truth. Only one who can see the entirety of reality, all the relevant facts of a given case, from a totally objective vantage point is qualified to sit as judge on matters of ultimate truth.

Wikipedia's opening definition, before going on to discuss a dizzying array of philosophical, theological and fact-based determinations of truth, says this:

*"**Truth** is most often used to mean being in accord with fact or reality, or fidelity to an original or to a standard or ideal.*

There's the rub. Is there an objective standard, a benchmark against which one can measure facts to determine truth? Is there an original source that gives definitive criteria by which to judge between veracity and mendacity? Who or what is the ultimate judge of reality? Where can one find a dictionary that specifically defines absolute truth?

In today's fallen world, truth is sacrificed on the altar of relativistic criterion, giving rise to phrases like *my truth* or *their truth.* The measure of truth becomes relative like the testimonies of the witnesses of the accident, based on a personal assessment of the *facts as I see them.*

Thankfully Christians have what albeit may be a simplistic answer to the question *"what is truth"* but it is also the only safe answer. Jesus said *"I am the Truth"*[4], taking the question out of the realm of religion or philosophy or subjective reasoning and placing it squarely in the realm of the absolute, the source and root of reality, God Himself. That being true, we can rest knowing that whatever Jesus says is the truth. We may look to Him for the answers to any and all questions regarding morality and ethics, specifically to find in Him the pattern by which we learn to walk this life of faith.

Further, we can agree that Jesus is and must be the final arbiter on any

---

[4] **Joh 14:6** Jesus saith unto him, I am the way, the truth, and the life: no man cometh unto the Father, but by me.

question of interpretation of **all** of Scripture, Old and New Testaments. He said "*I speak only those things my Father commanded me to speak*[5]". If He only said and did as His Father instructed Him, then the church is on solid ground to speak and do exactly as Jesus spoke and did.

The question you and I must answer then is this: what exactly did Jesus do? How did He conduct Himself on a daily basis? What was the standard by which He lived His life? What was the source of His understanding exactly what it was His Father spoke to Him and commanded Him to speak? The answer is clear to any who have an ear to hear and eyes to see.

1 WAS THIS TRUTH FOR ALL OR JUST THOSE FEW SPECIAL PEOPLE HE LIVED + SPOKE TO? — A DISPENSATION OF TIME.

2 WAS NEW TRUTH GIVEN TO SH'UL OR OTHERS AFTER HIM IN THE "CHURCH?" ... FOR THEIR DISPENSATION?

3 DOES EACH INDIVIDUAL GET UNIQUE TRUTH FOR THEIR UNIQUE GIFTS + CALLING?
  YES, BUT IT DOES NOT CONFLICT w/ TORAH + Y'SHUA.

HE WAS + IS JEWISH + THE WORD— CAN HE DO ANYTHING DIFFERENTLY? NO.

DOES HE HAVE ONE BRIDE OR MANY?

IS THERE ONE WAY, TRUTH, + LIFE?

---

[5] **Joh 12:49** For I have not spoken of myself; but the Father which sent me, he gave me a commandment, what I should say, and what I should speak.

2
WWJD

Christians young and old proudly display little rubber wristbands emblazoned with the letters WWJD, an acrostic for **W**hat **W**ould **J**esus **D**o.

That's actually a good question, albeit a moot one if we ask but don't intend to seek out the answer. Why ask if we're not willing to actually apply what we find? Why ask what Jesus would do and then ignore what it was that He did?

That's a bit like claiming to use a recipe for cornbread that calls for corn meal but refusing to read the ingredients and using desert sand instead. Gee! Wonder why it doesn't turn out?

Shouldn't we then, if we're honest about the question, do what He would do? That question **must** be answered if the Church is ever to rise to her true calling, speaking truth to power, being a light in the darkness, testifying to the truth of a loving God who is intimately involved in the daily affairs of His creation. As individuals, if we are honest about calling ourselves disciples of Jesus Christ, we must do a possibly brutal self-assessment and ask the hard questions. Questions like:

Are we really following in the footsteps of our Master?

Do we listen closely for His voice, attentive and obedient to the instruction of our Shepherd?

Do we love God with all our heart, soul, mind and strength?

Are we taking up our cross daily and following Him, crucifying the carnal nature, demonstrating His righteousness in an increasingly unrighteous culture? *STARVE THE FLESH, FEED THE SPIRIT, STRENGTHEN THE SOUL*

Do we love our neighbors in a way that reflects the light of God's grace?

Are we faithfully seeking to Do What Jesus Did?

What's Love Got to do With It?

It's all about love. Love is an action word. If love is real, there will be a demonstration of the reality of that love. A husband may speak the words *I love you* a thousand times, but as any wife can attest, the words ring hollow if there is no attendant action that shows the reality of the words. Most women would rather see a sermon than hear one.

The simplest definition of love comes from the mouth of Jesus. He said to Philip *"If you love me, keep my commandments."*[6] It doesn't get any simpler than that. If one truly loves the Savior, obedience to His will becomes a natural outgrowth of that love.

Just so there is no confusion about which commandments He referred to, read verse ten[7] from the same passage. The commandments Jesus kept and subsequently passed on to His disciples were obviously the ones His Father declared from the beginning. To think Jesus taught anything other than the commandments of His Father would be heresy of the highest order and no sane Christian I know would dare suggest such a thing.

Obedience Is Better Than Sacrifice
?INSULT TO MOST CHRISTIANS

A.W. Tozer said *"To escape the error of salvation by works we have fallen into the opposite error of salvation without obedience."*

The Scripture is clear. Obedience is better than sacrifice.[8]

---

[6] Joh 14:15 If ye love me, keep my commandments.
[7] Joh 14:10 Believest thou not that I am in the Father, and the Father in me? the words that I speak unto you I speak not of myself: but the Father that dwelleth in me, he doeth the works.

NOT THE BEST SCRIPTURE 7
1 JH 5:1-5

We are called to be a holy people, a people of righteousness, separated from the ways and motives of the world. We are a peculiar people, set apart to a life of obedience.

The question we face is obedience to what or to whom? Where do we look to learn specifically what it is our Heavenly Father expects of us?

Do we look to pastors or other leaders in the Church? They were placed in the Church to be examples of righteous living, as a conduit through which the life of Jesus could flow into His body and transform us all into His image. However, the fact is they are subject to human failure, just like you and I. That is not to say there is no place for leadership in God's House, but only to say each individual ultimately has a personal responsibility before God to seek Him out for themselves, lest we be deceived[9].

Do we just look to the Holy Spirit? The Bible does teach that the Holy Spirit would be the one to teach us all that Jesus said and did. However, Scripture tells us fallen angels are transformed into angels of light, speaking flattering words of lies and deceit. History is littered with examples of teachers who adopted a *me and the Holy Spirit* attitude and wound up teaching heresy that directly contradicted Scripture. Any word from any spirit that does not align with revealed Scripture is not and cannot be of the Holy Spirit and must be rejected.

A conversation:

"You must obey." "I obey" What do you obey? The Spirit. What does the Spirit tell you about adultery. Don't do it. How is that different from obeying the Commandment?

There **must** be a means by which one can see clearly what is expected, a working list if you will, specifically what is and is not acceptable behavior.

There is. It's been in your hands all this time.

---

[8] 1Sa 15:22 And Samuel said, Hath the LORD as great delight in burnt offerings and sacrifices, as in obeying the voice of the LORD? Behold, to obey is better than sacrifice, and to hearken than the fat of rams.
[9] 1Jn 3:7 Little children, let no man deceive you: he that doeth righteousness is righteous, even as he is righteous.

Turning Back – The Root of Repentance

Our entrance into relationship with God that elevates us to the sublime level of perfect righteousness[10] is attended by a requirement that is seldom ever preached from most pulpits. That is the word **repent.** God has been calling people to repentance since the day our first parents brought sin into the human domain.

The Greek word behind the English *repent (metanoeo)* has two parts: *meta* and *noeo*. The second part (*noeo*) refers to the mind, its thoughts and perceptions, dispositions and purposes. The first part (*meta*) is a prefix that regularly means movement or change. So the basic meaning of repent is to experience a change of the mind's perceptions and dispositions and purposes.

The Hebrew source of the English and Greek words for *repent* comes from the word שוב pronounced *shoov.* The few times the word is ever explained in most Christian circles, it is said to mean *"to turn around; to change directions"*, in other words, to turn away from sin. That is certainly a necessary part of repentance; however it fails to accurately describe what the word means *in the language God spoke when He defined it.*

JER 8:6 !!!

After all, wouldn't it be possible to turn around (from sin) but then simply head down a different wrong path again? A weak analogy would be that of a cigarette smoker *turning* or quitting smoking, only to replace that habit with one of gluttony. He's turned around, gone a different direction, but the new direction is just as damaging as where he came from.

The word literally means *"to return; to go back to the source"*, not just to **turn,** but to **return.** The word Sabbath comes from the same root, in essence meaning *"return to the covenant, the place of cessation of labor"*.

"RE-" IS BIG!

Being Sorry Is Not Repentance

Repentance is Biblically shown to be an internal change of mind and heart rather than mere sorrow for sin or mere improvement of behavior. Our

[10] **2Co 5:21** For he hath made him *to be* sin for us, who knew no sin; that we might be made the righteousness of God in him.

prisons are full of people who are sincerely sorry for doing the thing that got them their all-expense paid vacation. They are sorry not because of a moral change of heart. They're sorry because they have to pay the price for doing it.

Jesus points to this meaning of repent in Luke 3:8, describing the relationship between repentance and new behavior. It says, "Bear fruits *in keeping with* repentance." Then it gives examples of the fruits: *"Whoever has two tunics is to share with him who has none, and whoever has food is to do likewise"* (Luke 3:11). This means that repenting is what happens inside of us that leads to the fruits of new behavior. Repentance is not the new behavior but the inward change that bears the fruit of new behavior. The order is this: our heart changes because we have been saved, and because we are saved, our outward behavior reflects the inward change. Jesus is demanding that we experience this inward change, but then He expects us to show outward evidence of inward change. — HABITS, MINDSETS, RITUALS, COMFORT ZONES

The call to repentance is or should be a vital component of preaching the Gospel. It was important enough that the prophets of old thundered the message of repentance to God's people with a clarion call that still reverberates across the ages.

Noah preached repentance. Seven people and a bunch of animals got on the boat with him.

Enoch preached repentance and judgment came at the death of his son Methuselah.

John the Baptist preached a fiery message of repentance and it cost him his head.

The first demand of Jesus' public ministry was *repent.* He spoke this command indiscriminately to all who would listen. It was a call for radical inward change toward God and man. His demand for repentance was universally preached without prejudice, to self-righteous Pharisees and insufferable tax collectors; to humble fishermen and to the courts of power. None are exempt from Jesus's call to repentance.

If the preaching of repentance was critical in Jesus's ministry, why is it not a vital part of the message Christians hear on a daily basis? The message heard from today's pulpits, almost without exception, is a feel good, positive reinforcement, *be the best you that you can be* message, surely based on clear promises of God but devoid of any demands for a change in a person's heart.

↳ GRAFIE + MERCY.. + HOPEFULLY BLESSING

Obedience is not how high you jump during praise, but how high you exalt God in your praise.

↳ IT CAN'T BE FAKED + WORK, RIGHT?

Exuberant praise is a glorious expression of joy in the Lord and it is certainly commanded in Scripture. Which is exactly the point: obedience is a willingness to put feet to our faith and do what is instructed in God's Word.

Obedience means I am willing to see myself in the mirror of God's Word, to see myself as He sees me, and CHANGE! If faith does not change a person then how can that faith save a person?

Why? His answer is that we are sinners. *"I have not come to call the righteous but* sinners *to repentance"* Luke 5:32

Repenting means experiencing a change of mind that now sees God as true and beautiful and worthy of all our praise and all our obedience. This change of mind also embraces Jesus in the same way. Seeing God with a new mind includes seeing Jesus with a new mind.

VITAL TO HIS RETURN.

No one is excluded from Jesus' demand to repent. He made this clear when a group of people came to him with news of two calamities. Innocent people had been killed by Pilate's massacre and by the fall of the tower of Siloam (Luke 13:1-4).

Jesus took the occasion to warn even the bearers of the news: *"Unless you repent, you will all likewise perish"* (Luke 13:5). In other words, don't think calamities mean that some people are sinners in need of repentance and others aren't. *All* need repentance. Just as all need to be born again because *"that which is born of the flesh is [merely] flesh"* (John 3:6), so all must repent because all are sinners. He also was not saying there are those whose righteousness is such they don't need repentance. They are the ones who are trusting in their own righteousness

When Jesus said, *"I have not come to call the righteous but sinners to repentance"* (Luke 5:32), he did not mean that some persons are good enough not to need repentance. He meant some *think* they are (Luke 18:9), and others have already repented and have been set right with God. For example, the rich young ruler desired *"to justify himself"* (Luke 10:29) while *"the tax collector . . . beat his breast, saying, 'God, be merciful to me, a sinner!' [and] went down to his house justified [by God!]"* (Luke 18:13-14).

Therefore, no one is excluded. All need repentance. And the need is urgent. Jesus said, *"Unless you repent, you will all likewise perish."* What did he mean by *perish*? He meant that the final judgment of God would fall on those who don't repent. *"The men of Nineveh will rise up at the judgment with this generation and condemn it, for they repented at the preaching of Jonah, and behold, something greater than Jonah is here"* (Matthew 12:41). Jesus, the Son of God, is warning people of the judgment to come, and offering escape if we will repent. If we will not repent, Jesus has one word for us, *"Woe, to you"* (Matthew 11:21).

This is why the demand for repentance is part of his central message that the kingdom of God is at hand. *"The time is fulfilled, and the kingdom of God is at hand: repent ye, and believe the gospel."* (Mark 1:15). The gospel—the good news—is that the rule of God has arrived in Jesus to save sinners before it arrives at his second coming in judgment. So the demand to repent is based on the gracious *offer* that is present to forgive, and on the gracious *warning* that someday those who refuse the offer will perish in God's judgment.

After Jesus rose from the dead, he instructed his apostles to continue his demand for repentance in their preaching of the Gospel throughout the world. *Luke 24:46,47 "And said unto them, Thus it is written, and thus it behooved Christ to suffer, and to rise from the dead the third day: And that repentance and remission of sins should be preached in his name among all nations, beginning at Jerusalem.* (Luke 24:46-47).

The demand of Jesus to repent goes to all the nations. It comes to us, whoever we are and wherever we are, and lays claim on us. This is the demand of Jesus to every soul: Repent. Be changed deep within. Replace all God-dishonoring, Christ-belittling perceptions and dispositions and purposes with God-honoring, Christ-exalting ones.

Why so much emphasis on repentance, you ask? Obviously, God considers repentance to be of primary importance. It is the act of contrition that opens the door to God's matchless grace, the outward evidence of inward change that defines a true believer in Jesus Christ as Savior.

Repentance is the initial response of the sinner to God's offer of salvation. It is also an ongoing requirement to examine ourselves daily whether one is in need of repentance in any area of one's life. Repentance does not add to one's salvation. It is evidence of a changed heart, the fruit of having come into covenant relationship with the Lord of our salvation. It is the love response of one who desires above everything else to be pleasing to the Author of so great a salvation, who said *"Your sins are forgiven. Go and sin no more."*

SO CAN FORGIVENESS BE GRANTED WITH LIMITED TO NO REPENTENCE?

3

THE ME GOSPEL

The airwaves are awash with sermons that dwell on the grace of God without ever calling the listener to repentance, with never a word about sin or the deep brokenness in so many local congregations. The good news has been transformed into a *me* message with a focus on how I can be blessed, how I am favored of God, to seek the Kingdom of God for what I can get out of it.

The life-saving power of the Gospel message is so compromised in many of today's mega churches that at least one television preacher blatantly proclaims and finds broad acceptance that most ancient of all lies: *you too can be a God!*[11]

Another Church leader blasts his heresy shamelessly into millions of homes via satellite, saying Christians must have nothing to do with the Commandments of God if we are to have victory over sin in our lives. Emphasizing the point, he clarifies **even the big ten!**[12] What we find most

---

[11] *"You really cannot ever come to that place where you let this mind be in you which was also in Christ Jesus, who thought it not robbery to be called equal with God. Let this mind be in Kenneth Copeland, Oh my goodness, Ah! that thinks It's not robbery to be called equal with God."* – Kenneth Copeland, Believer's Voice of Victory, Monday 29th January 2001, GOD TV
"You're all God. You don't have a God living in you; you are one! … When I read in the Bible where God tells Moses, 'I AM,' I say, 'Yah, I am too!'" – 'The Force of Love,' Kenneth Copeland, tape BBC-56

alarming are the enormous crowds of trusting souls that flock to their meetings. They come seeking manna from Heaven only to be served a tainted self-serving message delivered right off the peak of Mount Blessme. They line up for a turn at the fount of the *slap me healed* healing line, then go home to the same lawless lifestyle that they were taught by the very shepherds who are even now picking their pockets and lining their own.

Is this the Gospel? Is this the Good News of Jesus Christ, Son of the Living God, Savior and Redeemer of mankind? Is this the message preached by His disciples or by Paul the apostle? Pray tell, is this the fruit of the Spirit manifest in our midst? Is it our calling to build massive edifices, seating thousands of adoring fans, while the homeless and the orphans and the widows cry alone? They beg for crumbs that might fall from the tables of these fabulously wealthy teachers, who live out their lives in mansions that would make European nobility salivate. Is this all there is? Multiplied thousands of our brothers and sisters in the Mideast watch while their babies are ripped from their arms and sacrificed under the blade of a most vile and treacherous Islamist *"religion of peace"*. Meanwhile, self-absorbed Christians in the West turn a blind eye to their plight. We're happy to funnel millions of dollars into the coffers of charlatans just for the chance at the Holy Lottery winning ticket, but please, don't bother us about actually heeding our Master's call to feed the poor; to clothe the naked; to rescue the helpless, both inside the womb and out. God help us. No! God help those who we will not help!

This is not the Gospel of Jesus Christ and deep in your troubled conscience you know it isn't.

Dear brother or sister, if you find yourself trapped in this deceptive ruse, think very seriously about what Jesus said in the following two passages. Remember, He is Truth, and nothing He says is without consequence.

> *Mat 5:17-19 "Think not that I am come to destroy the law, or the prophets: I am not come to destroy, but to fulfil. For verily I say unto you, til heaven and earth pass, one jot or one tittle shall in no wise pass from the law, till all be fulfilled. Whosoever therefore shall break one of these least commandments, and shall teach men so, he shall be called the least in the kingdom of heaven: but whosoever shall do and teach them, the same shall be called great in the kingdom of heaven."*

---

[12] Multiple teachings from Creflo Dollar

Mat 7:20-23 "Wherefore by their fruits ye shall know them. Not everyone that saith unto me, Lord, Lord, shall enter into the kingdom of heaven; but he that doeth the will of my Father which is in heaven. Many will say to me in that day, Lord, Lord, have we not prophesied in thy name? and in thy name have cast out devils? and in thy name done many wonderful works? And then will I profess unto them, I never knew you: depart from me, ye that work **iniquity.** *"*

For the record, you know that little word *iniquity* emphasized above? It's not what our preachers have been telling us for centuries. *Don't worry about it,* they said. *That's just talking about evil and wicked rapists, liars and baby killers,* they said. But what does the Bible say?

The Greek word is *anomos* and it literally means *lawlessness.*

G458 ἀνομία anomia an-om-ee'-ah

From G459**; illegality**, that is, **violation of law** or (generally) wickedness: – iniquity, X transgress (-ion of) the law, unrighteousness.

The word is used eight times in the New Testament. Following are the references in italics with commentary in brackets on each. The first is noted above, in which Jesus tells His disciples that there will be those who claim to believe in Him and do many impressive works in His name but are actually what we might call today *nominal Christians*, those who profess faith in Jesus but whose hearts are far from Him.

For the sake of clarity, in your own reading of the following passages, replace the word *iniquity* with the word *lawlessness* and see if they don't strike a chord of truth in your spirit.

> Mat 13:41 *The Son of man shall send forth his angels, and they shall gather out of his kingdom all things that offend, and them which do iniquity;* [Jesus here describes the end of the age when those who are saved are separated from those who are not. Those who are not saved are those who practice lawlessness.]

> Mat 23:28 *"Even so ye also outwardly appear righteous unto men, but within ye are full of hypocrisy and iniquity."* [This severe rebuke is directed at the religious leaders, those who insisted on placing the yoke of bondage of Torah-less tradition upon God's people. Christianity almost universally teaches that Jesus was rebuking the

Pharisees for making the people keep the Commandments. Nothing could be further from the truth. He was castigating them for **not** keeping the Commandments of God but rather teaching that their traditions equated to God's law, therefore walking in and teaching lawlessness.]

Mat 24:12 *And because iniquity shall abound, the love of many shall wax cold.* [Jesus was responding to the disciples' question about when He will return. His reply pointed very clearly to lawlessness as one of the defining characteristics of the time just prior to His return. The lawless, Christless society we live in couldn't be a clearer picture of what Jesus was alluding to. Mass murder of the unborn in the womb, partial birth abortion and sometimes live birth in order to preserve organs for sale for profit; re-defining marriage in blatant disregard for how it was defined by God *in the beginning;* sex-education in public schools with graphic illustrations in government mandated textbooks foisted on our children as young as age five; removal of all traces of Judeo/Christian ethics from public and scholastic arenas; all of which are clear signs of a culture that has lost its moral underpinnings. Ours is a sick and broken society and it is all a result of a pervasive anti-law culture. If Christ's Church teaches lawlessness, why would we expect society around us to behave any differently?]

Rom 6:19 *"I speak after the manner of men because of the infirmity of your flesh: for as ye have yielded your members servants to uncleanness and to iniquity unto iniquity; even so now yield your members servants to righteousness unto holiness."* [Clearly Paul makes a distinction between lawlessness *'iniquity unto iniquity'* and holiness that is the result of yielding our flesh to righteousness.]

2Th 2:7 *"For the mystery of iniquity doth already work: only he who now letteth will let, until he be taken out of the way."* [A reference to the lawless one to come, whose primary characteristic is a complete rejection of God's laws.]

Tit 2:14 *"Who gave himself for us, that he might redeem us from all iniquity, and purify unto himself a peculiar people, zealous of good works."* [Question: if He redeemed us from *lawlessness,* what are the *good works* Christians are zealous of if not the afore-mentioned laws of God?]

Heb 1:9 *"Thou hast loved righteousness, and hated iniquity; therefore God, even thy God, hath anointed thee with the oil of gladness above thy fellows."* [Quote from Psalm 45:7; if Jesus hated lawlessness, why would you and I think lawlessness is somehow a mark of distinction that identifies us as Christian?]

Think about the fact that there is one coming and suddenly will be revealed as the Man of Sin, the Lawless One.[13] Do we really want to align ourselves with the one whose manifest nature is to walk in blatant rebellion against God's Law and deceive others to do likewise?

If Jesus tells us to *"keep His commandments and teach others to do the same"*, and our teachers tell us *"don't keep the commandments"* and teach others to do the same, who do you think carries the weight of divine authority? Do we heed the voice of the liar, who was a liar from the beginning, or the one who is truth personified who said *"My sheep hear my voice and will not follow another … "*[14]

No, I'll tell you what we do. We hear the word *commandment* and our handy dandy automatic interpretizer kicks in. Suddenly the word takes on a sinister meaning, a tool that wicked Judaizers and legalists use to drag unsuspecting and trusting souls into the pit of a burning hell. Friends, just between you, me and the fence post, I think our Father takes a very dim view of shepherds who fleece His flock for their own benefit,[15] and to think it's happening in the name of the one who said He never changes!

It is an insatiable and voracious beast that has the audacity to stand before millions of trusting believers and declare with self-appointed authority *"Send*

---

[13] 2Th 2:3 Let no man deceive you by any means: for that day shall not come, except there come a falling away first, and that man of sin be revealed, the son of perdition;

[14] Jn. 10

[15] Eze 34:8-11 *As* I live, saith the Lord GOD, surely because my flock became a prey, and my flock became meat to every beast of the field, because *there was* no shepherd, neither did my shepherds search for my flock, but the shepherds fed themselves, and fed not my flock; Therefore, O ye shepherds, hear the word of the LORD; Thus saith the Lord GOD; Behold, I *am* against the shepherds; and I will require my flock at their hand, and cause them to cease from feeding the flock; neither shall the shepherds feed themselves any more; for I will deliver my flock from their mouth, that they may not be meat for them. For thus saith the Lord GOD; Behold, I, *even* I, will both search my sheep, and seek them out.

us a hundred dollars and God will bless you. Send us a thousand and by golly our Great ATM in the sky will just open up the Heavens and pour out monetary favor like rain." God's grace is cheapened to extend those empty promises in social media with promises like "Like *this and you'll be blessed.* Share *it and you'll be even more blessed!"* God is not your fairy godmother and that's not how blessings work! God will not be manipulated and His blessings are not for sale. **Grow up!**

How dare we? How dare we cheapen the message of God's matchless grace and merchandise it like some common commodity? If their premise is true, that giving to their ministry somehow opens the hand of God to favor you with multiplied monetary blessings, why not ask them to send a thousand dollars to every old person, widow, and young mother who has given into their ministry? Think of the untold riches that will pour into their coffers when God blesses them for their faithfulness. Would they do that? Do they trust their doctrine enough to do that? No? We didn't think so.

John F. Kennedy, in his inaugural address, January 20th, 1961, said *"Ask not what your country can do for you. Ask what you can do for your country."* Borrowing from Mr. Kennedy, as Christians we must *"Ask not what our God can do for us. Ask what can we do for our God?"*

All who buy into the lie of the enemy who first cast doubt on the eternal word of God with his challenge to Eve, *"Hath God said?"* should be asking themselves, not *"Do I know Jesus?"* but rather *"Does Jesus know me?"*

Source of the ME Gospel

The source of the *me* gospel is, well ... *me*! It's that ever-present personal pronoun that points directly to the essence of I, myself, a personal entity with self-will. Man alone has volition, the ability to make moral decisions, one of the primary characteristics that differentiate between man and animals.

Encoded within the name ADAM in Hebrew we see the essence of what it is to be man. Created in the image and likeness of God, man is imbued with potential to grow, to become more, to increase in expression of the image of our creator, endued with a divine spark of creativity that reflects that likeness. The image of God is reflected in the letters of Adam's name; *alef, dalet, mem* – A-D-M. The first letter, *alef,* represents God, the Singularity, the un-sourced source of all that exists. The letter alef depicts the connection between the spirit realm and the physical realm. The second part, *dalet mem* pronounced *dahm,* is the Hebrew word for blood. Where do we as unique individuals derive physical life? Our life comes from the blood, or DNA from both of our biological parents. Coincidentally, the numerical value, known as gematria, of the word blood is equal to the numerical value of the words for Father and Mother, giving us a hint of the nature of humanity and our connection to our creator.

On the other hand, behemah, the word for animal, has the intrinsic meaning of *in it is what it is*. In other words, an animal can never become more than it is, acting and reacting solely on the basis of instinct. Of course some animals can be trained, but an animal cannot make moral decisions or grow spiritually to behave better today than it did yesterday. It can only behave according to how it was programmed **in the beginning**.

In the human domain, ME-ism is as old as the Garden of Eden. Looking further back, we find the ancient founder of the ME-ist cult with his self-deifying *"I (me, myself) will be like the most high."*[16], the tempter who first infected Adam and Eve and by extension all of humanity with the genetic plague of sin.

What is sin? At its root sin is an attitude of independence, of going my own way, of doing my own thing, of self-expression rather than expressing and growing in the image of God. Ever since that fateful day in the Garden, man has battled with ME-ism. I want. I need. Me; My; Mine. Gimme. Gimme. Gimme. It's Sammy Davis Junior singing *"I did it my way"*. It's an egotism that sees itself as the center of the universe, with all of creation serving as a support system for *me*. MEism is an exaltation of the self, when God's will for man is that we crucify the flesh (the old, fallen self-nature); that we put off the old man and put on the new man which is created in Christ's likeness; that we manifest the fruit of His spirit which involves self-control, self-denial, an attitude of Christ exalting rather than self-exalting.

The most succinct definition of sin comes from the Bible itself. Who'da thunk it, right? *"Whosoever committeth sin transgresseth also the law: for sin is the transgression of the law."* 1 Jn 3:4

MEism in the Desert

What started on a whim in 1986 has grown to be the ultimate orgy of self-expression: BURNING MAN.

---

[16] Isaiah 14

Founder Larry Harvey and his friend Jerry James build an 8' wooden figure and drag it down to Baker beach along the California coast on the Summer Solstice. Setting it ablaze, a crowd gathered to watch it burn. Since that day the crowds attending the annual event in the Blackrock Desert in Nevada have grown, reaching numbers as high as 58,000 "burners". The leadership are even now seeking approval from BLM to expand the allowable number to 70,000. The size of the burning man effigy that is burned as the climax of the event grew as well, reaching heights north of 60 feet in some years.

On the splash page promoting the 2015 event we read *"Once a year, tens of thousands of people gather in Nevada's Black Rock Desert to create Black Rock City, a temporary metropolis dedicated to community, art, **self-expression**, and **self-reliance**. In this crucible of creativity, all are welcome."* [Emphasis mine]

"Immediate experience is, in many ways, the most important touchstone of value in our culture. We seek to overcome barriers that stand between us and a recognition of our inner selves, the reality of those around us, participation in society, and **contact with a natural world exceeding human powers**. *No idea can substitute for this experience."*

Emphasis of the preceding phrase begs the question: are there unseen forces motivating what seems to be a near universal cultural evolution toward glorifying the self, especially considering the choice to conduct the Burning Man event on the Summer Solstice?

The connection of Summer Solstice, sometimes called Litha, to pagan deity worship has a well-documented history. Having more daylight than any other time, Litha was considered to be a direct counterpoint to the darkness of Yule, the celebration of the Winter Solstice. The modern Christianized reformulation of the ancient pagan worship practice of the Yuletide is now better-known as Christmastide, or Christmas. One Wicca source has this to say, in case some feel they're not getting the full benefit from their version of this ancient rite. *"No matter where you live, or what you call it, chances are you can connect to a culture that honored a sun deity around this time of year."*

Here is a short list of historic deities celebrated on Litha, the Summer Solstice:

Amaterasu (Shinto), the solar goddess *"from which all light comes"* – Japan

Aten, an aspect of Ra, the chief sun god – Egypt

Apollo, son of Zeus – Greece

Hestia, goddess over domesticity and family – Greece

Horus, connected with Ra – Egypt

Huitzilopochtli, warrior sun god required worshipers to make regular sacrifices – Aztec

Juno, patroness of marriage; the month named for her and is popular time for weddings - Rome

Lugh, a harvest god similar to the Roman god Mercury – Celtic

Sulis Minerva, blend of Celtic sun goddess and Roman Minerva – Celtic & Roman

Sunna or Sol, Norse goddess of the sun - Germanic

Our forefathers understood very well the pagan roots of Christmas. It was banned in this country until 1836 when Catholic influence in the halls of power changed the course of American religious history. Today, Christians bristle at the mere suggestion that their venerated religious customs might have connections to ancient paganism. However, our Christian forebears had no problem taking a stand against attempts to incorporate worldly worship practice into their most holy faith. An excerpt from Fox News John Gibson's book The War on Christmas illustrates their efforts to keep the Church separate from un-Biblical traditions that have absolutely nothing to do with the Messiah, save in the minds of those who insist on defending them.

> *"As a matter of American history, however, some of the strongest complaints about the public celebration of Christmas have been lodged from within the Christian tradition—by devout Christians who had little use for the holiday. For a surprising number of American believers, the chief concern wasn't putting Christ back into Christmas. It was taking Christmas out of Christianity."*

Reasons for protests/riots in today's society usually center around complaints about income inequality, racial discrimination, real or perceived, and new to the entitlement feed trough, the cause celebre' of gender identity. Rioting is not new, but at least some riots were sparked for a much more theological reason. One Christmas day in Boston, crowds of angry Americans rioted in the streets. Two opposing groups scream angrily at one another, each side convinced of their moral high ground. The two groups meet. Accusations are hurled. Names are called. Words turn into shoves turn into fistfights. Mayhem ensues. Church windows are shattered, as are many a reputation. What social injustice are these groups fighting to correct? Christmas! They were fighting over or not to celebrate Christmas. One group, consisting mostly of Anglicans, Episcopalians and Catholics favors celebrating Christmas. The other group, made up of Baptist and Presbyterian followers, opposes all Christmas observances. This isn't an imaginary event, it is history. It happened in Boston on Christmas day in 1706.

Lest one think that was an isolated incident, the truth is the celebration of Christmas was abhorred by Christians almost across the board. One of Christianity's most revered and effective expositors of the Bible, Charles Haddon Spurgeon, had this to say:

> *"Those who follow the custom of observing Christmas, follow not the Bible but pagan ceremonies."* Sermon, Dec. 4, 1871

Having read all the preceding, if you dear reader are comfortable celebrating annual holidays that without controversy are rooted in ancient worship practices devoted to none other than Satan himself, that is your prerogative. As for me and my house, we chose decades ago to reject the Adversary's pagan holidays in favor of the eternal Holy Days of the Most High. At this late stage in world history leading up to the return of the King of Kings, I would beg Christians everywhere to "… finish the Restoration. Come **all** the way out of Mystery Babylon".[17]

---

[17] 2Co 6:14-18 Be ye not unequally yoked together with unbelievers: for what fellowship hath righteousness with unrighteousness? and what communion hath light with darkness? And what concord hath Christ with Belial? or what part hath he that believeth with an infidel? And what agreement hath the temple of God with idols? for ye are the temple of the living God; as God hath said, I will dwell in them, and walk in them; and I will be their God, and they shall be my people. Wherefore come out from among them, and be ye separate, saith the Lord, and touch not the unclean thing; and I will receive you, And will be a Father unto you, and ye shall be my sons and daughters, saith the Lord Almighty.

If you think I'm being harsh or insensitive by calling out the unquestionably pagan roots of Christian holidays, please ask yourself how you might react if you returned from an extended absence and found your husband or wife in bed with another person. Jesus expects to find followers faithful to His model when He returns, not a people intent on re-interpreting His word to allow for pagan celebrations under the guise of Christian terminology. Too extreme you cry? I have one phrase for you to consider: Golden Calf.

Come out from among them and be ye separate, lest you find yourself sharing in the plagues appointed to the non-believer.[18]

The 10 Principles of Burning Man

Burning Man co-founder Larry Harvey wrote the Ten Principles in 2004 as guidelines to reflect the newly-formed community's ethos and culture as it had organically developed since the event's inception. Listed here are three of the ten which we believe accurately define the spirit of Burning Man:

> **Radical Inclusion -** Anyone may be a part of Burning Man. We welcome and respect the stranger. No prerequisites exist for participation in our community.

> **Radical Self-reliance -** Burning Man encourages the individual to discover, exercise and rely on his or her inner resources.

> **Radical Self-expression -** Radical self-expression arises from the unique gifts of the individual. No one other than the individual or a collaborating group can determine its content. It is offered as a gift to others. In this spirit, the giver should respect the rights and liberties of the recipient.

All of this may seem innocuous enough. Until, that is, we understand the Devil's entire agenda is built around an ecumenical oneness of religion, education, government and financial system with self-expression at its core. Think New World Order.

---

[18] Rev 18:4 And I heard another voice from heaven, saying, Come out of her, my people, that ye be not partakers of her sins, and that ye receive not of her plagues.

An article by a Burning Man adherent makes a clear reference to the lawlessness of the movement with this missive titled <u>Does Wearing a Utilikilt and Fuzzy Boots Make You More Authentic?</u>

> *"Nobody gets authenticity points for following the 10 commandments: why should they get them for following the 10 Principles?"*

MEism in the Pulpit

ME-ism in the church has a name: *Hyper-grace*[19]

The past several decades have seen a dramatic decline in doctrinal and biblical preaching. We have gone from theology to therapy in the pulpits. Today one is likely to hear a feel good message from the pastor and never once be convicted of sin or be challenged personally for lacking fruit of the Spirit.

Gone are the days of fiery sermons from holy men of God like Leonard Ravenhill[20] or Keith Green, and more recently with the loss of David Wilkerson in an auto accident. They have all been replaced with motivational speakers in the pulpit with feel good messages that resonate with man's natural desire for self-expression but lack the fire of Holy Spirit conviction.

When was the last time you heard a message that made you squirm in your seat; made you blush for the sin suddenly revealed that was hidden deep in your heart; that shook you to your core with the realization of your own apathy concerning the things of God? Sadly, it rarely happens in today's American church.

---

[19] Evangelist Daniel K. Norris offers this succinct definition of hyper-grace. *Focusing solely on the grace of God without preaching the divine law, justice and judgment of God is unbalanced. Remember, John 3:16 doesn't just tell us that God loved us and gave his son to us, it also tells us we will perish unless we believe upon Jesus.*
It seems to me that we have created a culture in which God's law isn't just physically taken down from courthouses across the nation, but spiritually it has been removed from churches as well. What a shame!
[20] *"The early church was married to poverty, prisons and persecutions. Today, the church is married to prosperity, personality and popularity."* – Leonard Ravenhill

A.W. Tozer [1897-1963] said *"Christianity is decaying and going down the gutter because the god of modern Christianity is not the God of the Bible"*. Those are harsh words, but if they were true when he wrote them, do you think they are any less true today?

Many of today's local churches and preachers refuse to take a stand against sin and rarely if ever mention the need for repentance. Topics like hell and judgment are too harsh for modern sensitivities. Many of these same churches in some cases allow people to minister as worship leaders or as youth pastors and turn a blind eye to their involvement in immoral sexuality, drunkenness and other worldly pursuits.

The Prince of Hyper-grace

The darling of the hyper-grace message who rose to near rock star status in recent years is the wildly popular Joseph Prince, author of <u>Destined to Reign</u>.

It is not our place to judge another person's relationship with God. It is our job however to challenge errant teaching in the Body of Christ. The kneejerk response of many when defending their favorite Pastor/Teacher/Best-Selling Author is *"God tells us **not** to judge!"* Does the Bible say this? It does **not**!

What the Bible **does** tell us is not to judge by our own opinions but to judge all things by the word of God. In John 7:24 Jesus says: *"Judge not* **according to the appearance** *but judge righteous judgment."*

All of us make judgments every day; it's part of the process of decision making, of expressing that most unique of human experience we call free will. As Christians, we must learn to make judgments based not on emotion or personal opinion or on the opinions of those in leadership, but by the Word of God as His Spirit gives understanding.

God told Israel to judge the prophets in the Old Testament, whether they be true or false. The true prophets judged the false and called them out on their falsehood. Of course then as now people reacted strongly, saying the same things people are saying today. *"You're being judgmental." "Your message is negative." "Judge not lest ye be judged"* they said. We must consider the context in which Yeshua spoke those words. It's obvious He was speaking of hypocritical judgment, accusing someone else of the same things you yourself are guilty of. We're told in the New Testament to judge prophecy, to use discernment, to test the spirits. We are told to **test all** things. Why? Because it helps us discern what is right and wrong, to recognize falsehood from truth. It helps keep young believers who may be weaker in the faith from falling into error.

I realize that questioning one's favorite teacher or leader evokes a defensive posture and even a natural human response of anger in some people. But we must not use Scripture out of context to shirk our responsibility to hold one another accountable for our behavior or for false doctrine. What we believe determines our behavior. We should know clearly not only what we believe but why we believe it. Having our defense ruled by emotion is not advantageous in seeking truth but is in fact counter-productive.

It is an easy escapism from that responsibility to react with words like *"don't judge"*, *"touch not my anointed"*, *"do my prophets no harm"* and other equally spiritual catchphrases any time something is said about one's favorite teacher. Understanding these verses *in context* would eliminate most such flawed arguments and prevent us from emotional entanglements. Rightly dividing the Word is not just finding a few passages to prove a position. Anyone can do that. The real test is to know what they mean in context and how they apply to us today.

What is ironic is that to tell people they are judgmental is itself a judgment. Telling someone they are judgmental is essentially telling them to dispense with any discernment, to simply let God decide who is right and who is wrong. That sounds very spiritual to an immature mind, but it is contrary to everything God tells us in His Word about mutual accountability within the Body of Christ.

Ephesians 5:11 tells us not to have anything to do with works of darkness but rather to reprove them, meaning to confute, admonish, convict, convince, tell a fault or rebuke falsehood. Clearly it was Paul's opinion that we are to challenge falsehood, not hide behind Scripture taken out of context to justify easy escape from our obligation to truth.

Paul gives further warning about the double-sided sword of the goodness and the severity of God to the Roman believers.[21]

---

[21] Rom 11:22 Behold therefore the goodness and severity of God: on them which fell, severity; but toward thee, goodness, if thou continue in his goodness: otherwise thou also shalt be cut off.

The purpose is not to bring condemnation but to bring a brother or sister to repentance and restoration.

Consider 2 Thess. 3:14-15:

> *"And if anyone does not obey our word in this epistle, note that person and do not keep company with him, that he may be ashamed. Yet do not count him as an enemy, but* **admonish him as a brother.***"*

In that spirit, let us look briefly at some of the glaring examples from Mr. Prince's book that demand Biblical refutation.

> *The bottom line is that* **the Holy Spirit never convicts you** [a believer] **of your sins...***I challenge you to find a scripture in the Bible that tells you that the Holy Spirit has come to convict you of your sins. You won't find any! The body of Christ is living in defeat because many believers don't understand that the Holy Spirit is actually in them to convict them of their* **righteousness in Christ.** *Even when you fail..."*Destined To Reign, pages 134, 135

> *"Repentance and confession of sin are never necessary."*Destined to Reign, Pg. 53

Wow! It's hard to know where to begin addressing those blatantly flawed statements. They quite simply turn Scripture on its ear. John the Apostle gives stark warning to those who deceive themselves with this lie. Note his use of the first person plural pronouns *we, our and us,* indicating the subjects of the admonishment are believers.

> 1 Jn. 1:8-10 *"If we say that we have no sin, we deceive ourselves, and the truth is not in us. If we confess our sins, he is faithful and just to forgive us our sins, and to cleanse us from all unrighteousness. If we say that we have not sinned, we make him a liar, and his word is not in us."*

Obviously, John is speaking under the inspiration, you guessed it, of the Holy Spirit! Clearly the Holy Spirit convicts us of sin and Scripture is replete with examples of His calling believers to repentance. It is true that the Holy Spirit is in us to convict or to convince us of our righteous **standing** in Christ. It is also true however, that the Holy Spirit convicts us of our unrighteous **state** when we sin. The former is the result of faith in the finished work of Calvary's grace. The latter is a reflection of our moral

28

condition at any given point during the ongoing process of sanctification. One is faith based, the other is works based. We are saved by grace and we are *"being saved"*, that is morally perfected, by works. One is a gift of eternal life; the other is how we are rewarded in the world to come based on how we lived in this life. Both have eternal consequences, as Paul so eloquently describes:

> 1Co 3:13-15 *"Every man's work shall be made manifest: for the day shall declare it, because it shall be revealed by fire; and the fire shall try every man's work of what sort it is. If any man's work abide which he hath built thereupon, he shall receive a reward. If any man's work shall be burned, he shall suffer loss: but he himself shall be saved; yet so as by fire."*

The Father convicts believers of sin.[22] Jesus convicts believers of sin.[23] The Word convicts believers of sin. The Holy Spirit testifies for the Father and the Son.[24] The Holy Spirit teaches the Word. Ergo, the Holy Spirit convicts believers of sin and the need for repentance.

Numerous other examples in Scripture teach that the Holy Spirit is involved in Church discipline to confront, rebuke, correct and convict believers of sin and errant doctrine. Ananias and his wife Sapphira learned this harsh lesson when they lied to the Holy Spirit.[25]

---

[22] Heb 12:5 And ye have forgotten the exhortation which speaketh unto you as unto children, My son, despise not thou the chastening of the Lord, nor faint when thou art rebuked of him:
Heb 12:6 For whom the Lord loveth he chasteneth, and scourgeth every son whom he receiveth.
Heb 12:7 If ye endure chastening, God dealeth with you as with sons; for what son is he whom the father chasteneth not?
Heb 12:8 But if ye be without chastisement, whereof all are partakers, then are ye bastards, and not sons.
[23] Rev 3:19 As many as I love, I rebuke and chasten: be zealous therefore, and repent.
[24] Joh 15:26 But when the Comforter is come, whom I will send unto you from the Father, even the Spirit of truth, which proceedeth from the Father, he shall testify of me:
[25] Act 5:1 But a certain man named Ananias, with Sapphira his wife, sold a possession,
Act 5:2 And kept back part of the price, his wife also being privy to it, and brought a certain part, and laid it at the apostles' feet.
Act 5:3 But Peter said, Ananias, why hath Satan filled thine heart to lie to the Holy Ghost, and to keep back part of the price of the land?

Apostle Paul, by inspiration of the Holy Ghost (II Peter 1:21), instructed both Timothy (II Timothy 4:2) and Titus (Titus 1:13 & 2:15) to confront, rebuke, correct, and convince rebel church members of sin and false doctrine; therefore, if it is appropriate for conviction of sin to come through man by inspiration of the Holy Spirit, then conviction of sin is a work of the Holy Spirit

The human conscience is where conviction of sin takes place (John 8:9; Romans 2:15; etc.) and the Holy Spirit speaks to man through his conscience (Romans 9:1; I John 2:20); therefore, when man needs to repent, conviction of the Holy Spirit takes place

Sermon on Tap

What would Jesus brew? Water, wine, beer — what's the difference, right? Now, I'm not opposed to someone downing cold ale on a hot day. Or even a warm draft on a cold day for that matter if that's what floats your boat. But serving beer in church to attract potential converts? Seriously? It's true. Some local churches turn to serving beer to attract young seekers.

The idea of pack-a-pew Sunday rises, or should I say sinks to a whole new level.

Act 5:4 Whiles it remained, was it not thine own? and after it was sold, was it not in thine own power? why hast thou conceived this thing in thine heart? thou hast not lied unto men, but unto God.
Act 5:5 And Ananias hearing these words fell down, and gave up the ghost: and great fear came on all them that heard these things.
Act 5:6 And the young men arose, wound him up, and carried him out, and buried him.
Act 5:7 And it was about the space of three hours after, when his wife, not knowing what was done, came in.
Act 5:8 And Peter answered unto her, Tell me whether ye sold the land for so much? And she said, Yea, for so much.
Act 5:9 Then Peter said unto her, How is it that ye have agreed together to tempt the Spirit of the Lord? behold, the feet of them which have buried thy husband are at the door, and shall carry thee out.
Act 5:10 Then fell she down straightway at his feet, and yielded up the ghost: and the young men came in, and found her dead, and, carrying her forth, buried her by her husband.
Act 5:11 And great fear came upon all the church, and upon as many as heard these things.

Phil Heinze of Calvary Lutheran Church in Fort Worth, Texas, says *"I'm interested in having people have significant relationships around Jesus"*, referring to their unorthodox initiative to find ways to reverse the decline of church membership in recent years. *"And if it turns out to be craft beer, fine."* Combining Spirit with spirits, worship leaders hold communion at the bar and even sing hymns and songs of praise. Heinze said the idea is to spark curiosity in those around.

"Holy water: More and more churches across the country have taken to serving up pints — or even holding theological discussions at the local pub." Keith Srakocic/ASSOCIATED PRESS

NPR's The Salt blog carried an article called the The Strange Brew of Religion and Alcohol - and how it's attracting unexpected people to Christianity. Strange brew or strange fire – always sure to draw a crowd in any age.

First Christian Church parish in Portland, Oregon sponsors a similar event called Beer & Hymns once a month, with around a hundred young people swigging beer and singing praise to Jesus. They keep the "spirit" in check by limiting imbibers of holy brew to a two beer maximum.

Since the year 2000, a ministry in New York called Theology-on-Tap NYC, centered on microbrews and craft beers, takes the Gospel message of salvation to the unorthodox setting of an Irish pub.

The group says on its website that it is *"in perfect alignment with the Pope,"* explaining that the Holy Father commands that the Gospel of Christ should be taken to where the people are.

Happy Hour starts at 7:30 P.M. at Connolly's Bar on W. 45th St. in Manhattan every Sunday. After all, doesn't the Bible say somewhere happy is the man who sits in the company of sinners? The apostle Paul must have had this generation in mind when he wrote: *"Do not be idolaters as some of them were; as it is written,* 'The people sat down to eat and drink and rose up to play." 1 Corinthians 10:7. He also said "… *flee from every appearance of evil."* But then, it may be too much to ask of this generation to insist on a literal application of the Word of God. Times change; presentation of the Gospel message should change to keep pace seems to be their mantra.

Winning souls to Christ, one pint at a time. The world spins off its spiritual axis and our answer is to offer them more of what they already have. Surely it can't get any worse, right?

Tattoo and a Sermon

The spectator culture of modern Christianity, at least in the West, has become an insatiable monster. Church hoppers in days past changed Churches over disagreements with leadership, squabbles over the color of carpet in the new sanctuary or any number of other eternally insignificant pretexts.

Today's worshipers are presented with a smorgasbord of entertainment from which to choose, from rock music to dazzling stage productions. This is the stuff that adds numbers to the Church membership rolls. If you don't like Newsboys, Chris Tomlin is appearing down the street. Come one come all. And don't forget your tithes! Somehow, it seems what happened in Vegas forgot to stay in Vegas. Sadly, it's quite frankly difficult to tell the difference between a Church service and a rock concert. It's all about the entertainment. Whoever has the best entertainment fills the most pews.

There are reports of at least one or more Churches providing opportunity for worshipers to get a tattoo onstage during the sermon. Because after all, broken souls in today's world need that little extra push for the altar call to really work. Jesus and tattoos; yeah, those go together like mosquitos and a barbeque.

The God who created the universe with a word; who exchanged glory for flesh; who walked among us in an amazing life full of miracles; who willingly suffered the most ignominious death imaginable to pay for the sin of mankind; who then did the impossible, what no man in history had ever done before. He rose from the grave. He defeated death and the grave and with a shout of victory ringing through the halls of Heaven, He promised that you and I and all who trust Him would also be raised from the dead at His triumphant return ... all of that and people need an extra push?

But if someone gets a tattoo onstage during the sermon – yeah, that'll make the Gospel message believable. If only John the Baptizer had known!

"I didn't understand repentance before. But now that some guy got a tattoo during the sermon, I get it!" Yeah. Okay. And I have some Kool Aid for refreshment while you watch.

Leonard Ravenhill, a true prophetic lion of the previous generation, nailed it when he said *"The early church was married to poverty, prisons and persecutions. Today, the church is married to prosperity, personality and popularity."* p 25

Pastors, if you continue compromising with the world and acceding to the whims of popular culture, where will it end? If you say people are different today, that we need a gimmick to get people to church these days, you're playing right into the enemy's hands. Tickling ears and placating impatient pew warmers with every diversion under the sun might pack the pews, but it will also block the one thing they desperately need: confrontation with a Holy God and His demands for repentance. Besides, if people come to church because their services are contemporary and culturally relevant, what kind of people are we attracting? If we're competing with secular entertainment to draw a crowd, how long before that crowd moves on to a bigger and brighter spectacle? We absolutely **must** return to preaching the simplicity of the Gospel message and stop using the world's ways to win the world.

Me and You and LGBTQ and I Too

I woke up one morning recently and unbeknownst to me – but beknownst to someone somewhere, I'm sure -found I had been secretly transported to a weird alternate universe. Same bed. Same room. But the world outside my windows had overnight become clouded with a sickly green fog. Echoes of Rod Serling's opening narration flood my mind as I watch the country I love spiral into a cesspool of moral rot.

> *There is a fifth dimension beyond that which is known to man. It is a dimension as vast as space and as timeless as infinity. It is the middle ground between light and shadow, between science and superstition, and it lies between the pit of man's fears, and the summit of his knowledge. This is the dimension of imagination. It is an area which we call ... The Twilight Zone.*

For those still stuck in the ancient vernacular of 2015, let me bring you up to speed on how the initials for deviant lifestyles has evolved. Most of us know the LGBT stands for lesbian, gay, bisexual and transsexual. What has been added is the *"Q"*, which stands for queer - yes, they now proudly wear that moniker – and *"I"* which stands for *"Identity"*, short for how a person self identifies as a gender other than the one they were born with. Legitimizing gender fluidity with laws demanding acceptance of this travesty added fuel to the fires of perversion and opened the door to all manner of opportunities for claiming intolerance and offense. Everybody is offended these days. Well, guess what happens when someone is offended? Nothing! The offended person doesn't develop scabies. The Earth doesn't spin off its axis. The Walking Dead are still walking. Everything continues just the way it did before one is offended. So get over yourselves already! Adding to the lunacy, we now have white people who self-identify as black, grown men self-identify as little girls, transgender bearded women suckle babies that they themselves gave birth to. Yes, it really happens. And it really doesn't matter who is offended when those who practice this abomination are called to account. God in Heaven is offended and offending Him has enormous consequences. Something really does happen when He is offended and the world really will spin off its axis if we don't change our ways.

The Problem With The ME Gospel

On July 28th, 1982, the Church lost one of its anointed prophets. Keith Green and two of his children died in a plane crash shortly after take-off from their ministry property in Garden Valley, Texas.

A man on fire with the Gospel message, he was consumed with calling believers to holiness and challenging rampant hypocrisy in the Church. Following are excerpts in italics from a tract he wrote called **What's Wrong With the Gospel**.

> **It's Me-Centered Instead of Christ-Centered:** *First and foremost, it is the gospel that appeals to the selfish. Instead of honoring God, it places the sinner at the center of God's love and plan. But the Bible places Jesus at the center of God's plan, **not** the sinner.*

> *One of the most well-known phrases of modern evangelism is* "God loves you and has a wonderful plan for your life!" *But the sober, biblical truth that needs to be presented to the sinner's mind is* "You have made yourself an enemy of God, and in your present state of rebellion there is absolutely no hope for you." *In fact, God's* "plan" *for the sinner at this point in his life is to separate him from His presence forever, in hell. However unpopular or unlovely that may sound, it is the only truth and reality about anyone who is an enemy of God through sin.*

> *The whole line of reasoning in our modern gospel continues on and on in this mistaken way. "Sin has separated you from God, 'and His wonderful plan for your life.' Jesus came and died on the cross, so that you may experience*

'His wonderful plan for your life.' You must accept Jesus now, so that you will not miss out on 'His wonderful plan for your life!'" **You, you, you, you!!! It's all for YOU!** *I'm not sorry to say this, but Jesus did it all in obedience, for His* **Father's** *glory. (Phil. 2:8-12) Of course, it infinitely benefits those who love, serve, and honor Him, but that was a secondary consideration, not the primary one. (Please read Ezek. 36:22-32.) If people come to Jesus mainly to* **get** *a blessing, or only to* **get** *forgiveness, they will ultimately be disappointed. But if they come to* **give** *Him their lives in honor and worship, then they will truly have forgiveness and joy - more than they could ever imagine! (I Cor. 2:9)*

The Law of God Preached to Convict One of Sin. *Pages could be written on this subject, but there is room for only one brief example. When the rich young ruler came to Jesus, he asked a very direct question: "Good Master, what must I do to inherit eternal life?" Can you imagine what our preachers would answer him today?* "Just admit you're a sinner, accept Jesus as your Personal Savior, go to church, pay your tithes, try to be good, and you're in!" *But what was Jesus' answer? "You know the commandments... if you wish to enter into life, keep the commandments." (Matt 19:17; Mark 10:19) The commandments?? Why they went out with Cecil B. DeMille! Isn't this the "age of grace"?*

Well, the truth is Jesus wasn't preaching the commandments to him as the way of salvation, He was using the commandments to specifically convict him of his particular sin - greed. That rich boy loved the bucks, and Jesus knew just how to flush him out of the bushes - preach the Law! And that's exactly what the Law is for- "For through the Law comes the knowledge of sin" (Rom. 3:20), that's what Paul said. The Law must be preached - not as the way of salvation, but as a searchlight put on the sinner's heart, so he can see how utterly rotten he is, compared to the way God requires him to be. (Gal. 3:24)

But today again, we are wiser than God. Our preaching isn't filled with "dos and don'ts." No, we don't want to scare the "liberated generation" away. Why, if we said that fornication was wrong, or drugs, or abortion, or any other specific sin, people would feel all condemned and then how could they get saved? But that's just it, Jesus preached the Law to the rich young ruler so that, after feeling condemned about his greed, he could turn and obey Jesus and find true treasure in heaven. "Go and sell all you possess and give it to the poor, and you shall have treasure in heaven, and come, follow Me." (Mark 10:21) Unless people are truly convicted of sin, if they do not fully see that they are totally condemned by the requirements of God's Law, then it is

35

virtually impossible to show them the need for a savior. Why, what would they need to be saved from? Fun?

That is why our modern gospel must dwell on "all the good things God'll do for you if you'd just accept Him!" We can't convince a sinner that he needs a savior by just getting him to admit that, "Well, generally, yes, I am a sinner." He must see how the Law of God totally condemns him as a sinner, and then the beauty of the Gospel, the glory of the cross, the marvelous power of Christ's blood will be able to penetrate his anxious, waiting mind and heart. Only by the preaching of the Law can a man fully desire to be saved from his sin. For, "I would not have come to know sin except through the Law."(Rom. 7:7)

Green nails it with his strong admonitions in this tract over thirty years ago. The same message needs to be heard today. This is nothing new. For centuries the body of Christ has wrestled with antinomianism (*anti* carries the meaning of against or instead of, in place of; *nomos* means law). This is the belief that the law of the Old Testament has been done away with, and that, once we are in Christ, there is free grace in which we can live any way we want since we are not under law but under grace.

A phrase often used by hypergrace Christians-I'm embarrassed to have espoused it at one time-now that we're under grace says *"as a Christian you can do anything you want to but your want to has changed"*. That may sound pious and full of faith to some, but frankly, it sounds like the excuse of a wayward child that refuses to respect the wishes of his parents. The fact is, I am **not** allowed to do anything I want to and to suggest such a thing is a travesty of everything God's Word has stood for since time immemorial. I'm not talking about *"losing your salvation"*. I'm talking about wood, hay and stubble.[26] I'm talking about playing fast and loose with the holiness of God and that my friends, is a dangerous pursuit.

According to this view the Old Testament has no relevance to the New Testament Christian except for metaphors and types that point to the coming of Christ. Certainly, Psalm 25 is good material to quote at a funeral

---

[26] **1Co 3:12-15** Now if any man build upon this foundation gold, silver, precious stones, wood, hay, stubble; Every man's work shall be made manifest: for the day shall declare it, because it shall be revealed by fire; and the fire shall try every man's work of what sort it is. If any man's work abide which he hath built thereupon, he shall receive a reward. If any man's work shall be burned, he shall suffer loss: but he himself shall be saved; yet so as by fire.

when someone is walking in the valley of the shadow of death. Passages like *"Trust in the LORD with all thine heart; and lean not unto thine own understanding. In all thy ways acknowledge him, and he shall direct thy paths"*[27] make for good sermon material, however, what is conveniently left out is verse one, the foundation and first cause of the blessing, the repentance half of the equation for trust. *"My son, forget not my law; but let thine heart keep my commandments:"*

Paul the apostle warned against this un-Biblical idea in Romans 6:1-2 when he rhetorically asked: *"shall we continue in sin that grace may abound?"* His response: *"God forbid! How shall we that are dead to sin live any longer in it?"*

Yet we are taught that the Ten Commandments have little or no bearing in the life of the New Testament believer in spite of the fact they are taught directly and indirectly in the New Testament. Examples of the law being taught are Ephesians 6:1-3, a reference to the fifth commandment; James 2:11 quoting the sixth and seventh commandments; Romans 7:7 has Paul quoting the tenth commandment regarding covetousness; Paul also says that we dishonor God when we disobey the law (Romans 2:23).

Obedience to the Ten Commandments is also taught indirectly in 1 John 5:21 which instructs believers to stay away from idols (from the second commandment regarding not to make a carved image to worship); and when Jesus said that the greatest commandment in the law is to love God with all the heart, soul and resources (Matthew 22:37-38) which corresponds to the first commandment regarding having no other gods before Him. Paul makes it clear in Romans 7:12 that the law is holy, righteous and good and that the purpose of being filled with the Spirit of Christ is so the righteousness of the law would be fulfilled in us[28], not just so we can drift through life as spiritual beings, doing as we please, without any standards for obedience and righteous behavior.

We are indeed spiritual beings, but we have a very direct responsibility in this body of flesh to bring every thought and action into **obedience** to Christ. Paul wrote that he willed that we be sanctified spirit, soul and body. Put succinctly, we were set apart in the spirit, we are being set apart in our souls, and we will be set apart in the body - past, present and future. [See 2

---

[27] Proverbs Ch. 3

[28] Rom 8:4 That the righteousness of the law might be fulfilled in us, who walk not after the flesh, but after the Spirit.

Cor. 1:10] Our physical life in this world is the *soul* part in the process of sanctification.

Paul summarizes his entire theology with respect to the Commandments in one overarching comprehensive statement. Most Christians are only too eager to disregard and skim right over this verse, but we **must** take it into account when using his writings to develop our interpretation of Scripture. Read it prayerfully. It can change your life!

> Rom 13:9 *"For this, Thou shalt not commit adultery, Thou shalt not kill, Thou shalt not steal, Thou shalt not bear false witness, Thou shalt not covet; and if there be any other commandment, it is briefly comprehended in this saying, namely, Thou shalt love thy neighbour as thyself."*

There it is folks. The Church's favorite Apostle, the one whose quotes are used (misused?) to prove the law has been done away with, telling you and me the Commandments are for us, the New Testament believer. If we love God with all our heart, we'll love our neighbors; and if we properly love our neighbors, we will be fulfilling all the Commandments, not doing away with them.

Although we cannot be saved by following the law-everyone is guilty of breaking the law according to Romans 3:23-God uses the law as the standard of righteousness by which sin is exposed in us. Thus the law doesn't save us but it sanctifies us when we yield to the power of the Holy Spirit dwelling in us, as it is by the law we have the knowledge of sin.[29]

So then, to what does Paul refer when he says that we are justified apart from the law (Romans 3:21) through grace as a gift (Romans 3:24)? The context of these statements and the other teachings of the New Testament regarding the law are clear: while the law doesn't save us, it is still in effect as a guide and standard for righteous behavior.

Signs of a Hyper-Grace Church

With apologies or maybe thanks to Jeff Foxworthy, the following are signs that you might be in a hyper-grace church:

---

[29] Rom 3:20 Therefore by the deeds of the law there shall no flesh be justified in his sight: for by the law is the knowledge of sin.

- If your pastor never speaks against sin … you might be in a hyper-grace church.
- If your pastor speaks about sin only in the context of forgiveness of sins in Christ but never in the context of taking a stand against sin, you might be in a hyper-grace church.
- If your pastor only talks about the sins of legalism and Phariseeism to denigrate ministers who preach against sin in obedience to the Scriptures … you might be in a hyper-grace church.
- If your pastor never takes a cultural stand for righteousness … you might be in a hyper-grace church.
- If your pastor shies away from subjects like abortion or same sex marriage and is unwilling to make a public stand on cultural issues of morality … you might be in a hyper-grace church.
- If your pastor preaches from the Old Testament only as types and shadows for sermon illustrations but teaches it has no real value regarding our standard of living today … you might be in a hyper-grace church.
- If your pastor only preaches positive motivational messages on health, wealth, prosperity, God's love, God's forgiveness and on how to succeed in life … you might be in a hyper-grace church.
- If people who live immoral lives are allowed to lead ministries … you might be in a hyper-grace church.
- If key members of the church are regularly living sinful lives with impunity with no accountability … you might be in a hyper-grace church. *exemption from punishment*

Albert Einstein said *"The world is a dangerous place, not because of those who do evil, but because of those who look on and do nothing."* Not saying anything about immorality is tantamount to condoning it. Is it possible America is wallowing in a pit of decay and immoral decadence today because of the Church's silence on moral issues in the public arena?

It is our contention that the New Testament and Old Testament are organically connected with the New building upon the Old, not eradicating it as is commonly taught.

There is nothing inherently wrong with positive messages. Even a message of reproof can be given with a positive spin, not to make it palatable but to show the benefits of living God's way. We must remember: it takes two to tango. There is another side to the coin. A bird with one wing will fly in circles. It takes two oars to make progress in a boat. We must preach the message of grace but we have to be careful to preach the whole counsel of God and feed the flock a balanced diet instead of just the sweetness of feel-good messages. The grace of God is the way of salvation but the law of God is what forces us to look to God's grace.

Those attending a hyper-grace church will most likely find that, because of the strong emphasis on grace, with no teaching against sin or on repentance, judgment or hell, there is an atmosphere of loose living with many involved in habitual sexual immorality, drunkenness or other fleshly vices. Why? Because "*the law is our schoolmaster that leads us to Christ*" (Galatians 3:24) and because through the law comes the knowledge of sin (Romans 3:20). If we do away with the schoolmaster; if the moral law of the Ten Commandments is not preached or alluded to because it's been done away with, then in ignorance the people will live foolishly and blindly follow leaders who themselves are blind. Why? Because: "*Where there is no prophetic vision the people cast off restraint, but blessed is he who keeps the law*" (Proverbs 28:18).

One of the greatest dangers of the hyper-grace message is that it is a short step to universalism, the belief that all people will eventually be saved, whether they believe the gospel or not, e.g., Love Wins by Rob Bell and many prominent modern preachers.

Contemporary liberalism that is being imposed on all levels of society, with more and more of Scripture being eviscerated because it is culturally offensive, has become the norm for much of the world's population. In the rush to political correctness, inclusiveness and tolerance some universities are offering a list of alternate phrases to refer to individuals in non-gender specific terms, replacing offensive terms like her, him, he and she with bizarre made-up words like ze and xyr. You can't make this stuff up! If it wasn't so crazy one would have to laugh. There is even a new Bible called the Queen James Bible with all references to homosexuality removed; and why not? Once Scripture is stripped of its divine authority, i.e. parts removed or re-interpreted to fit any meme that happens to be in vogue at the time, it becomes a lifeless document subject to change on a whim and its Author a capricious demiurge.

The meme that has taken the world by storm since the latter half of 2015 is that homosexuality is a perfectly normal lifestyle and should be not only tolerated but accepted by the rest of the population. I just watched in amazement an ad on a PBS station, on the morning of November 12th, 2015. In it, the father of a child feeding him cereal and speaking in the voice of Darth Vader of Starwars fame says *"I am your father"*. The camera pans to the other side of the child to his other father who, speaking in the same voice says *"No. I am your father"* to which the first man says *"That was a terrible Darth Vader"* and everybody laughs. I was shocked! Sodom has indeed gone mainstream in modern society.

Dear God, send your Spirit; our nation is doomed without you!

Sadly, rather than effect change in our culture, the Church has absorbed much of the unrighteous mentality of society with a *"go along to get along"* attitude.

I believe antinomianism is a dangerous and ancient doctrine in evangelical Christianity that the Church and the world are reaping the fruit of. It is something we need to lovingly but strongly take a stand against with our brothers and sisters who espouse it.

Dr. Michael Brown talks about this contemporary gospel in charismanews.com, the internet version of Charisma magazine:

> *"The New Testament gospel starts with God and tells us what we must do to please Him. The contemporary gospel starts with us and tells us what God can do to please us. No wonder we are in such spiritual confusion and moral malaise."* [30]

> *"The biblical message of grace is wonderful, glorious and life-transforming. We can't live without it for one second of our lives. But there is a message being preached today in the name of a new grace reformation, mixing powerful truth with dangerous error. I call it hyper-grace."* [31]

> *"One of the foundational doctrines of the hyper-grace message is that God does not see the sins of his children, since we have already been made righteous by the blood of Jesus. That means that the Holy Spirit never convicts believers of sin, that believers never need to confess their sins to God, and that believers never need to repent of their sins, since God sees them as perfect in his sight."* [32]

Really? Is it true that one never needs to confess sins before God or repent

---

[30] Michael Brown; Confronting the Error of Hyper-grace; CharismaNews, 2/18/2013
[31] ibid
[32] ibid

of sins? What utter nonsense! Scripture would demand otherwise.

If that is true, why did Jesus rebuke five of the seven churches He referenced in chapters two and three in the book of Revelation? Especially consider His words to the assemblies at Ephesus and Sardis[33].

Why did He often conclude an encounter with those who came to Him for forgiveness with the words *"Go and sin no more"*?

Why did Paul the apostle have so much to say about repenting of sins within the Body?[34]

If it is true that God no longer sees our sins, why would John the apostle write in 1Jn 1:8 *"If we say that we have no sin, we deceive ourselves, and the truth is not in us. If we confess our sins, he is faithful and just to forgive us our sins, and to cleanse us from all unrighteousness. If we say that we have not sinned, we make him a liar, and his word is not in us."*?

It is out of the infinite kindness of God and His great love that He rebukes[35] us, not condemns us. Because sin is so destructive, nothing less than perfect grace can deliver us, as Paul says in Tit 2:11,12 *"For the grace of God that bringeth salvation hath appeared to all men, teaching us that, denying ungodliness and worldly lusts, we should live soberly, righteously, and godly, in this present world;"*

Tragically many Christians today mistake the voice of God's correction for the condemnation of Satan. How sad it is then when they resist the purifying work of the Spirit, claiming that there's nothing to purify since God no longer sees their sins. We ask God to work in our lives and as soon as the Holy Spirit convicts us of something needing correction, we rebuke the devil. The devil may be doing just what he is supposed to do: accusing the brethren. The difference is when God points to sin in our life it is for

---

[33] Rev 2:4 *Nevertheless I have somewhat against thee, because thou hast left thy first love.* And *Remember therefore how thou hast received and heard, and hold fast, and repent. If therefore thou shalt not watch, I will come on thee as a thief, and thou shalt not know what hour I will come upon thee.*

[34] 1Co 11:30-32 For this cause many are weak and sickly among you, and many sleep. For if we would judge ourselves, we should not be judged. But when we are judged, we are chastened of the Lord, that we should not be condemned with the world.

[35] Heb_12:6 For whom the Lord loveth he chasteneth, and scourgeth every son whom he receiveth.

the purpose of building up our most holy faith. When the enemy does it, it is for the purpose of tearing it down; same disclosure, different goal. One is conviction, the other is condemnation. Either way, if there is something in your life that needs fixing, fix it! Repent of it and move on. And **then** rebuke the devil.

Has God justified us by the blood of Jesus? Absolutely. Has He set us apart as a holy people unto Himself? Without a doubt. Has He called us to be His sons and daughters, all by His love and grace? Yes, He has. And it is because of these things that Paul wrote, *"Since we have these promises, dear friends, let us* **purify ourselves from everything that contaminates body and spirit, perfecting holiness out of reverence for God"** (2 Cor. 7:1). [Emphasis mine] It is a lofty and sacred calling. Don't let anyone steal it from you.

4

STILL I WILL FOLLOW

I Have Decided To Follow Jesus

Pentecostals and Baptists, Lutherans and Methodists, Christian denominationalists of every stripe have all probably sung this old hymn at one time or another. With heartfelt sincerity we sing the refrain *no turning back, no turning back.*

We listen to countless sermons, attend seminars and conferences galore. We share endless Bible studies on what it means to be a disciple of Christ. One would think we'd get it by now. But do we? Do we *get it*? Who or what are we really following? How are we, the Christian Church, doing in the area of making and being disciples of the master? Are we reproducing disciples in His image or are we spitting out converts in our own image with lawlessness as the foundation of their new life?

We're fond of quoting Paul, "*... be followers of me as I follow Christ*"[36], but rather than emulating Jesus, we find most of us are following Paul. Rather a version of Paul that he himself might not even recognize.

Peter said Paul's words would be **hard to understand and twisted (misinterpreted) by those who don't know the rest of Scripture.**[37]

---

[36] 1Co 11:1 Be ye followers of me, even as I also am of Christ.

[37] 2Pe 3:16 As also in all *his* epistles, speaking in them of these things; in which

Most of Christianity teaches by creed and by practice that Paul was sanctioned to preach the Gospel to Gentile believers, one that was distinct and separate from the *old* Jewish religion which was based on harsh laws given by a demanding Heavenly Judge. Friends that concept is taken right out of the creeds of Gnosticism. Gnostics taught that the God of the Old Testament, the *Jewish* God, was harsh and unbending, demanding strict obedience to a set of laws that humans are incapable of keeping – a common comment from many insisting that Jesus had to come and keep the law, since no one else is capable of it. Gnosticism teaches that Christ, the demiurge, was the first of God's creation, used by the Almighty to extend the work of creation.

The commonality of doctrine shared by all pseudo-Christian cults is based on the errant belief that man by his own fallen human cognitive prowess can explain the paradox of the nature of Jesus. In trying to reason through the Biblical truth that He is fully God and fully man, one eventually hits a conundrum. How can God be a man on the earth with all the frailties and brokenness of humanity and still be God in heaven? We either accept the truth by faith on the basis of the one who said it, or we default to our fallen logic to interpret the words of the one who said *"My ways are not your ways and my thoughts are not your thoughts"*. Is. 55:8,9.

It is Greek philosophical thinking that insists on bringing infinite truth down to the level of finite human comprehension in resolving seeming contradictions in the Bible, incongruities like *"God is not a man ..."*[38] and *"... thought it not robbery to be equal with God"*[39] You can't do it! How can finite human logic understand the infinite mind of God? His thoughts are higher than our thoughts. His ways are higher than our ways. We may apprehend

---

are some things hard to be understood, which they that are unlearned and unstable wrest, as *they do* also the other scriptures, unto their own destruction.

[38] Num 23:19 God is not a man, that he should lie; neither the son of man, that he should repent: hath he said, and shall he not do it? or hath he spoken, and shall he not make it good?

[39] Php 2:5-8 Let this mind be in you, which was also in Christ Jesus: Who, being in the form of God, thought it not robbery to be equal with God: But made himself of no reputation, and took upon him the form of a servant, and was made in the likeness of men: And being found in fashion as a man, he humbled himself, and became obedient unto death, even the death of the cross.

by faith what He chooses to reveal, but we cannot and will not fully comprehend the mind of God.

For example, Mormonism teaches that Jesus is the spirit brother of Lucifer and that He attained Godhood by keeping the commandments and ordinances of the Gospel (as the LDS church defines them).

Jehovah's Witnesses teach he is *"a"* god but not the supreme God. The only question that needs answering here is this: if Jesus is *"a"* god, doesn't that make him a false god, since there is only one true God? But if he is a false god, then doesn't that disqualify him from being savior and Messiah? However, to claim that he is a true God and indeed the savior of mankind, but not the Almighty God, you now have two true gods, albeit one is a lesser god. Now you've admitted to having **more** than one god. You can't have it both ways. It is linguistic suicide to say there is only one true God but there are two true Gods; a logical inconsistency to insist that there are two firsts and two lasts. [Cp. Isaiah 44:6, 8 with Rev. 22:13]

Human reasoning which makes the Word of God contradict itself in any way invariably leads to doctrinal errors. Bishop Arias of Alexandria was a key proponent in the spread of this gnostic gospel in the early church.

The sixty four thousand dollar question that must be asked is which Jesus are you following?[40] The road is broad and the gate is wide that leads to destruction. The single common denominator of doctrine shared by all false religions and pseudo-Christian cults is the rejection of the deity of Jesus, a key doctrine of Gnosticism. That road is built on the corroded foundation of improper interpretation of Scripture, making Scripture say what they believe rather than believing what the Scripture says.

Of course Jesus kept the law perfectly. Of course no one of us can keep the law perfectly. Of course we are not saved by keeping the law. But is that why Jesus kept the law, just so we wouldn't have to keep it? Really? Is that what the Scriptures teach?

Beloved, I submit to you that Jesus kept the Law because to do otherwise

---

[40] 2Co 11:4 For if he that cometh preacheth another Jesus, whom we have not preached, or *if* ye receive another spirit, which ye have not received, or another gospel, which ye have not accepted, ye might well bear with *him.*

would have been so totally perverse to his nature that the very thought would have been abhorrent to him, let alone disqualifying Him as the promised Messiah. The multitude of prophecies foretelling his appearing point to a savior who delighted to do his Father's will.[41]

The example he leaves us is one of righteous living by walking in obedience to the laws of His Father. This is the way Jesus shone as the light of the world. He lived and breathed the Word. His claim to be the light of the world was qualified with expectancy in the disclaimer *"While I am in the world ..."*Jn. 9:5.

He conferred that obligation to shine upon you and me, the Church. Matt. 5:14, 16 *"Ye are the light ... Let your light so shine that the world will see your good works ... ".* Jesus here points to works, not words but works, the righteous behavior of the redeemed as the light that the world will see. To follow him is to walk as He walked, to behave as he behaved, to speak as he spoke. Jesus shone as the light of the world by keeping His Father's commandments. It is incumbent upon you and me, if we are to take seriously Jesus's command to take up our cross and follow him, to be disciples and not just converts. The Church will shine brightest when we with one voice cry out in repentance and begin to walk as Jesus walked.

We asked in a previous chapter, what exactly did Jesus do? And if we are to shine with the same intensity, by doing what he did, what is it we should be doing to shine his light in a dark and darkening world? Here's a short list of the things he did. I believe those that have an ear to hear will be quickened by the Holy Spirit to hear the word of truth.

If you're following at the Biblical Jesus - there is another Jesus according to Paul[42] - you'll find He:

- Kept Torah (Logical, since he wrote it)
- Observed the seventh day Sabbath
- Kept the Feasts of the Lord according to Leviticus 23

---

[41] Ps 40:8 I delight to do thy will, O my God: yea, thy law is within my heart.
[42] 2Co 11:4 For if he that cometh preacheth another Jesus, whom we have not preached, or if ye receive another spirit, which ye have not received, or another gospel, which ye have not accepted, ye might well bear with him.

- Ate only foods designated as clean according to His Father's Word
- Taught Torah in the synagogues
- Taught Torah **after** His resurrection
- Demanded that Torah violators repent
- Never bowed before any idol
- Honored all the commandments
- Never asked for or expected money from those who "walked the aisle"
- Never celebrated a pagan holiday
- Opened blind eyes, healed the sick, fed the hungry, raised the dead and
- Did more miraculous works than could be detailed in a thousand volumes
- Why? Because he delighted to follow his Father's commandment to do so

Gnosticism in the Church

Gnostic teaching goes on to say the New Testament God, Jesus, was much kinder and gentler, full of grace and truth, unlike the God of the Old Testament whose great delight was making such severe demands for obedience that no one could live by. The law was given to show us we can't keep the law. Tell me how that makes sense; how a loving God would devise plan A to tell his people to do something he knew they were unable to do, only to then offer plan B? This idea is so ingrained in the modern Christian Church, a phrase overheard in a church service perfectly sums up the underlying sentiment of this wholly unbiblical view: *"the church needs the son to protect them from the Father"*. We've been taught that the Son is the counterpoint to the Father, that vengeful Old Testament Judge demanding obedience to unlivable rules and meting out justice with thunder and lightning.

Does the Bible teach that the laws were too hard to keep therefore Jesus came to the earth to keep them so we wouldn't have to? And do we think that since we are under grace, obedience to God under the direction of the

Holy Spirit is somehow different from obedience to God when it's written on tables of stone? Is keeping a commandment that is written by the finger of God on tables of stone organically different from keeping the same commandment written by the finger of God on your heart? It is baffling how Christians will keep the Ten Commandments in daily practice but insist they're not keeping the commandments. A precious Saint who would cringe at the thought of stealing something but at the same time insist they're not keeping the commandment against stealing seems double-minded. How is eschewing the sin of adultery in obedience to the law written on your heart different from keeping the same commandment written on stone? To insist it's because on the one hand it is done under the law but on the other it is under grace is utter confusion.

1 Cor 3:1-1?

As a matter of fact, <u>most Christians delight in obedience to all of the Commandments</u>, even while rejecting the principle of *"keeping the law"*. <u>All that is save one: the fourth.</u> There are myriad interpretations used to reject keeping of God's seventh day Sabbath, from teaching the Bible simply means to set aside any day of the week as your Sabbath to posit that God changed the Sabbath from the seventh day to the first day at the other end of the hermeneutical spectrum. Again, utter confusion based on interpreting the Bible to fit a pre-conceived belief rather than on clear teaching of Scripture, in my opinion.

Here's what the Bible really says: *"The secret things belong unto the LORD our God: but those things which are revealed belong unto us and to our children forever, that we may do all the words of this law."* Dt. 29:29

Since Jesus is the final arbiter of proper interpretation of Scripture, let's see what He says:

Matthew 5:17-19 *"Think not that I am come to destroy the law, or the prophets: I am not come to destroy, but to fulfil. For verily I say unto you, Till heaven and earth pass, one jot or one tittle shall in no wise pass from the law, till all be fulfilled. Whosoever therefore shall break one of these least commandments, and shall teach men so, he shall be called the least in the kingdom of heaven: but whosoever shall do and teach them, the same shall be called great in the kingdom of heaven."*

Many of you are at this point rushing to find passages of Scripture to prove Jesus didn't mean what it looks like he said. So let us focus on what he did say in this passage and the actual meaning of the words he chose to use.

The meanings of two words in this passage are critical to proper interpretation:

Destroy - *kataluo* meaning *"destroy, dissolve, come to nought, overthrow, throw down"*

Fulfill - *plerosai*, meaning *"to fill, complete, fully preach"*

Much of the Church's doctrinal teaching that the believer in Christ is now *"not under the law"* – a phrase we will focus on later – is supported by the claim that by *"fulfilling the law,"* Jesus did away with it, making it irrelevant to the believer.

If we allow the verse to simply say what the verse says, we find:

- The word *plerosai* (fulfill) **does not** mean *to "do away with"* or to *"overthrow."*
- The word *kataluo* (destroy) **does** mean to *"do away with"* or to *"overthrow."*
- Jesus emphasizes in verse 18 that heaven and earth would pass away before the tiniest part of the law (Torah) is done away with.
- Finally, consider carefully what he says **to believers** at the end of this verse. He is not referring to the Godless heathen who reject him. He's speaking directly to you and me, to his blood-bought disciples, saying if we break the least of his commandments and teach others to do so, we will be considered least in the Kingdom of Heaven.

Jesus is clearly teaching that his fulfilling the law in no way diminishes the authority or the ongoing validity of the law. He explains the fuller meaning of the Torah, teaching his disciples to not only keep the Law, but to see beyond the letter of the Law, to understand the Godly principles behind the commandments, or the spirit of the law.

Example: The law says *"thou shalt not commit adultery"*. According to Jesus even looking upon a woman with lust is adultery in the heart, a more stringent demand that reflects the spirit of the law. He *fully preached*, or properly interpreted the law, which is the meaning of *fulfill*.

I submit that *"every Word that proceedeth out of the mouth of God"* means that your pastor is lying to you if he says the instructions of YHVH have been abolished, and that in fact Jesus confirmed this.

I contend that **if** Paul changed God's Word, he is guilty of gross heresy, of adding to and taking away from the Word, which was **explicitly** prohibited in the Old Testament[43] as well as in the New Testament.[44] If Paul was promoting a Jesus who did not keep Torah, His Father's words, then he is presenting a false Messiah who forfeits his claims of prophetic fulfillment. Paul would be guilty of teaching *another Jesus,* one that neither he nor the other Apostles preached; one who proved himself to be *another* Jesus.

The true Messiah, the one expected by pious Jews, would be one who kept Torah perfectly, down to the very last jot and tittle. Is it any wonder we seem almost totally incapable of winning our Jewish friends to Jesus when we present a blonde-haired blue-eyed savior who instructed the Apostle Paul to change what His Father instructed Him to say and do? Sadly, and much to our and their detriment, many anti-missionary Rabbis use the same misinterpretations of Paul's writing to prove that very point; that he was responsible for starting this new religion called Christianity with a lawless savior at the helm. Using Christianity's own spurious hermeneutics, they've been very effective in not only hindering many Jews from accepting their Messiah, but also in convincing great numbers of Christians to forsake belief in Jesus as the Savior.

Most Christians give token agreement to the Jewishness of the Savior and the Gospel message, yet insist Paul changed all that as having no relevance to the believer in Christ's new church. Since Jesus kept all the laws perfectly, we are somehow absolved from keeping any of the laws. The prominent preacher referred to earlier who brazenly opined that to have victory in this life a Christian should have nothing to do with the law, specifically calling out **the big ten,** is a poster child for the hypocrisy of this

---

[43] Deu_4:2 Ye shall not add unto the word which I command you, neither shall ye diminish ought from it, that ye may keep the commandments of the LORD your God which I command you.

[44] Rev 22:18 For I testify unto every man that heareth the words of the prophecy of this book, If any man shall add unto these things, God shall add unto him the plagues that are written in this book:

MEism.

What audacity! What hypocrisy, for him and others of his ilk to teach on the one hand that God did away with all the laws and on the other hand to teach (enforce?) the one law sure to keep their coffers full, their mansions maintained, and their Lear jets fueled and ready for the next fleecing. Their attitude seems to be that of the bandito Calvero in the 1960 movie The Magnificent Seven, *"if God didn't want them sheared, he wouldn't have made them sheep."*

If the law is done away with, why keep the law of the tithe? The answer seems self-evident.

Dear friends, if you are caught up in that blab it and grab it gospel, RUN! Run as fast and as far away from that deception as you can get! Judgment begins in the house of God and He always starts at the top. He is not going to deal kindly with those who to this day make His Father's house a house of commerce.

If Paul actually taught the law is abolished, he is promoting *another Jesus* and *another gospel*, which Paul himself said is anathema![45]

This begs the question: what exactly does it mean to follow Jesus? How do we conduct ourselves in the Church today in a way that reflects Jesus's demands for holiness in our lives?

Here it is in a nutshell. When Paul said *"be ye followers of me as I am of Christ"*[46] the word *follower* in Greek is μιμητής which means imitator. In other words, imitate me because I imitate Christ and in imitating me you are imitating Christ.

You and I share an unbroken chain of discipleship back to the Savior Himself. Every saved person on the planet came to know the Savior as a result of the witness of another disciple that came before. How sad that we in the Church talk a big talk of following Christ but rarely go beyond our spoon-fed doctrine to walk out the concept behind what he meant when he

---

[45] Gal 1:9 As we said before, so say I now again, If any man preach any other gospel unto you than that ye have received, let him be accursed.
[46] 1Co 11:1 Be ye followers of me, even as I also am of Christ.

said follow me. To follow Rabbi Jesus is to be like Rabbi Jesus; to think like him, talk like him, believe like him, and behave like him. It means to imitate him in every way as he leads us by his example and his word.

So the question remains: who is the Church following? Are we following Jesus, imitating him, doing the things he did, believing and behaving as he did? Or are we following the Church Fathers, theologians and religious leaders who early on began to interpret Scripture with a decidedly antinomian bias?

 It will be shown in another chapter that they, the Church Fathers, adopted an agenda, one whose primary purpose was to separate the Church from anything to do with *Jewishness*.

Suffice it to say, we have come to a crossroad in history as this age winds down. Will we follow our example Jesus or will we continue down a road of lawlessness disguised as grace, regurgitating doctrine of lawless teachers in defense of our own rejection of God's law? In the words of Jesus, **repent.** Come back to your first love. Take up your cross and follow him.

Go and Make Disciples

Of all the things Jesus said when He walked this earth, there are few as powerful as His statement *"Come. Follow Me."* From that short statement arises the heart of what it means to be a Christian. It is a call to become a disciple. What an amazing invitation! What grace! The maker of the Universe just asked you if you would trust Him to make of you something infinitely beautiful out of what is irreparably broken without Him!

We've developed a culture that is fixated on church growth, on numbers. Many churches boast a tally board in the back of the sanctuary showing how many converts they've "won", how much money was tithed and other supremely important spiritual necessities of Christian life. That's the problem. We're making converts, not disciples. We're creating duplicates of ourselves, lawless converts that look like us but don't look anything like Jesus.

Most of what passes for the Gospel today is a preacher preaching a hyper grace message of God's love and forgiveness without ever requiring repentance on the part of the seeker. Common practice in most churches follows a pattern. First there is an altar call, an invitation to accept Christ followed by the all-important walk down the aisle, symbolic of an outward show of sincerity. Then, following the pastor in a pat prayer, one is assured of eternal life, followed by encouragement to be baptized and join the church. Not THE Church, but to put your name on the membership rolls of the local assembly. How many seekers follow this pattern and never come into relationship with the living God; who never come face to face with their own sinful nature and how utterly repugnant it is to the Holy One? Friends, you can pray that prayer of salvation a thousand times and never experience the New Birth; you can be baptized a thousand times and still come up a wet sinner – for the thousandth time – and not be changed from the inside out.

Baptist Evangelist Paul Washer tells of a farmer attending one of his meetings. The man, who was dying of cancer, was convicted deeply and took the preaching to heart, realizing that all men are dying under the weight of sin and that he personally needed forgiveness. The man was well known in the community as an upright individual, a man of honor and integrity. However, he stumbled at trying to understand how his own sins could be paid for by another. While the rest of the church was engaged in the time-honored tradition of the Potluck after the meeting, Brother Washer spent hours ministering to him after the sermon, sharing Scripture after Scripture, truth after truth, until finally the man read for the umpteenth time *"God so loved the world …"* and with tears streaming down his face sobbed *"I get it! I understand! Have you never read what it says here? I'm saved! I know I'm saved!"*

We do the seeker a disservice and the Gospel an injustice when we preach a message devoid of any responsibility on the part of the sinner. Does that mean he can't be saved until he repents? Doesn't that make his salvation one of works? Look at it this way. Grace is God's offer of a marriage proposal; repentance is the response saying *"I do"*. The repentance is the willingness to turn from what God says is unholy as a result of the salvation by grace that is offered without reservation, no strings attached. If one is truly born again, one's behavior will reflect the change in the new creation.

Volumes have been written on the subject of Christian discipleship. Songs have been sung, poems written, entire ecclesiological movements were founded under the banner of the discipleship/mentoring principle. The question that faces us, you and me, is – how are we doing with this discipleship thing? Is the church making converts or disciples? Are we reproducing disciples who are conforming to the likeness of Jesus, or are we making pupils that are clones of ourselves, who in turn are replicas of the Church Fathers and their wrong-headed traditions of lawlessness?

Crisis of Adulthood

Everyone is going to follow someone. Even a self-made man worships his creator.

We have a crisis of manhood in America today. Great numbers of our boys grow up without a clear picture of what it means to be a man. Many inner city boys are raised without a father in the home, finding acceptance in street gangs of their peers. Many others are raised by harsh, judgmental Fathers with impossible to meet standards, never feeling accepted and approved of by their first and most important role model. Emasculated and effeminate, this generation manifests a bizarre social phenomenon called *gender fluidity*. Individuals are encouraged to self-identify as whatever gender they choose to be, regardless of nature's physical endowment. The personal pronouns he and she are becoming passe' and even discouraged in conversation. Gender confusion is moral confusion. Shocking but not at all surprising given the moral state of a country bent on removing every vestige of the Absolute standard of morality, God's Law. What is surprising is how Christians can be outraged at the sin that pervades our culture and not once consider the fact that the Laws of God were discarded by the very Church that should be demanding obedience to those laws. We follow man's laws by the tens of thousands without even a blink of the eye. But the mere mention that we are beholden to the Laws of God elicits a barrage of accusations of *"you've gone back under the law"* or *"you've fallen from grace."* Go figure.

There are two primary reasons for the modern crisis of manhood.

One is a culture of male denigration which developed in Western countries, beginning in earnest when the concept of feminism forced itself into public consciousness. Rights without responsibilities, equality of outcome is the goal. TV programming consistently portrays men as weak, effeminate, doltish, without authority, ruled by a smart wife, disrespected by his children. Demand for equal rights has become our banner cry. America is consumed with rights, the right of blacks to be recompensed by a generation that had nothing to do with slavery; of women to equal pay regardless of whether she performs as well or produces as much as her male counterpart; right of gays to marry, right to free education, right to a living wage (whatever that is), free food, free cellphone, free free stuff. In today's topsy-turvy social paradigm, men demand the right to use the women's bathroom in public places, individuals have the right to be a woman in a man's body; grown men self-identify as a six year old girl. Yes, this really happened! The opportunities for self-expression are limitless. Be a party penguin if that's what trips your trigger. The absolute mind blower is that this behavior finds acceptance among the population. The meme seems to be whatever floats your boat, just do it.

With no apologies, I say NO! God is still a Holy God and He still demands holiness in a people, any people, who desire to live in a peaceful and morally responsible society. The voices of the prophets thunder through the ages to condemn this generation for its wickedness. We'd better prepare ourselves to walk alone in the righteousness of God than walk with the majority that is destined for judgment. There is one word that needs to spill from the mouths of believers to this generation; one word, whether believers call themselves Christian, Hebrew Roots, Messianic, Protestant – the one word that needs to be proclaimed with conviction rooted in the authority of God's Word – REPENT!

The other reason for male identity crisis in this writer's opinion is adolescence that extends much later in a young man's life than in previous generations. Thought to end in the twenties at the latest, men are extending their adolescence much later in life.

The fault may be in large part because of a culture in which rites of passage have all but disappeared, except for a few indigenous cultures. Boys are left adrift and lost, never sure when and if they've become men. Today's men lack a community of males to initiate them into manhood and to recognize their new status. Oh, there is no lack of peer support to point a boy to what this generation perceives as manhood. When does a boy become a man? What is the marker that determines manhood? Is it when he first has sex? Any boy once he reaches puberty can produce a child. It's well said any boy/man can father a child, but it takes a real man to be a Dad.

Is it when a boy is eligible to vote he becomes a man? Is it when he gets his first job, pays taxes, graduates high school, goes to war, gets married? All of those may be valid societal markers of adulthood, but I daresay none of those truly are able to define a path to maturity.

Historically, cultures worldwide have inherently understood that without clear markers on the journey to manhood, transitioning from adolescence to adulthood is difficult. Rites of passage were clearly defined in most cultures as important rituals that served as the doorway of recognition and acceptance into the community of adult males.

While rites of passage varied greatly from culture to culture in how their ceremonies took place, there was a commonality of experience that involved emotional or physical pain and commitment to his appointed task. The test of manhood allowed the young candidate to show courage, endurance, and his determination to learn to handle the challenges of adult life.

> *Modern society has provided adolescents with no rituals by which they become members of the tribe, of the community. All children need to be twice born, to learn to function rationally in the present world, leaving childhood behind.*

> *In another place or time, you might leave your village to go onto the Mountain for as long as it takes. Animals speak to you, lightning crashes around you, the sun bakes you, and the wind separates the chaff of childhood from the living seed of your new life. Discovering your place in the greater web of things, you offer thanks for your gift and return to share it with your people. Having moved through adolescence, you take up your new place as an adult in your clan. You are worthy of a chance to gain their respect. Your quest has shown you a new purpose and a vision of what your life can be.*

> *We might send our children alone into the desert to wander alone for a year, dead to us--except that we pray often for them. They learn the plants, the animals, the water holes, the power places, and the songs. Praying alone at the center of the world, they glimpse a new chapter in their stories. With this gift, they come back to us, bringing spiritual renewal and wisdom. Our songs and celebration welcome them for we know that their rite of passage has nourished us as well as them. In turn, our celebration confirms to them that something vital has happened. Their flames burn brighter. Leaving as children, they return as adults just as we did years before.* Bill Moyers, quoted in Cohen, 1991, p. 45)

The rites of passage serve to preserve cultural ideals and a connection from generation to generation to its indigenous social order.

We in the West do celebrate important social milestones with events such as graduation exercises, confirmation, bar and bat mitzvahs, weddings, anniversaries and such. However, these events fail to seal the connection of the individual to his or her societal obligations. Oftentimes they are empty rituals and the individual simply goes through the motions to please someone else.

We can get a clearer understanding of the importance of rites of passage by considering the ceremonies of many native American tribes as they celebrated the passage from adolescence to manhood. The movie <u>A Man Called Horse</u> showed a graphic scene of the film's hero, played by Richard Harris, as he undergoes the ritual of manhood in order to be inducted into the Sioux Tribe. In the gruesome scene, Harris has ropes attached to his chest by means of a pair of eagle's claws dug into his flesh, with the other ends of the ropes connected to a pole. Others have events like it, albeit perhaps not quite so ghastly. A boy goes into the woods and sits overnight blindfolded, bearing the dread of hearing every screech, scrape, growl and other terrifying sounds in the night forest air. Meanwhile, his father is sitting on stump nearby, watching over him while he deals with his own emotions during his night of testing.

Other cultures have a multitude of ceremonies to mark a rite of passage. You may remember a time when your whole family gathered to watch you and another kid from the next neighborhood beat the living *bleep* out of each other with whips while relatives and neighbors cheered. And then nobody called the cops. If so, you probably grew up among the North African Fulani tribe (or in certain parts of New Jersey).

A Fulani boy becomes a man by engaging in an epic battle of self-control with a boy from a rival clan. The sharo ritual involves two young boys facing each other in a ring, both shirtless, both carrying a long cane or whip. The boys then take turns smacking the *bleep* out of each other by striking the opponent three times across the ribs and back as hard as they can. The whole tribe gathers to watch the battle and cheer them on to victory. The winner is chosen by the crowd. The winner is the one who opens the deepest bloodiest wounds on his opponent while flinching less when his own insides are exposed to the open air.

A rather gruesome test of manhood so let's not go there. Where we can go however, is around the world to an ancient time when the ultimate rite of passage came with the words ***follow me.***

5
I BELIEVE IN YOU

Those Were the Days My Friend

Seems the older people get the more **they** reminisce about the *good old days*. Bunyan-sized nostalgia seems to be a common affliction of older folks, too. Yes, I said *they*, second person plural pronoun, to distinguish between them and us don't suffer those evocative sentiments. Adventurous souls with a creative bent may even attain prominence in the science community for having discovered heretofore unknown laws of physics i.e., see next paragraph.

You remember those days, right? There was a daily five mile walk to school and back home again, uphill both ways in hundred degree weather with two feet of snow on the ground. This was a common experience for children in those days, one whose character building benefits are lost to today's technology constrained culture. My siblings and I got character that way, although character building may have suffered somewhat due to the simultaneous development of the art of truth stretching. Note the second sentence of this paragraph for example.

It was a time when we had to actually wade through six inches of shag carpet to change channels on the TV set. That is, if your parents even owned a television set. Some of us had to earn a place on the couch and God forbid nature's call should force you to relinquish your cherished vantage point. The vacuum created by your absence sucked another body into position quicker than Marshal Dillon could draw down on a bad guy! Then, like now, we were force fed annoying fifteen minute sales pitches in between short segments of show time pegged at decibel levels heard in the next county. Some things never change.

Back then, kids had a vast playground all to themselves. It was called *outside*. We climbed trees and rode bikes without helmets and tumbled in the dirt as we wrestled and built up our physical strength as well as our immune system, all without benefit of a gym. In today's technology bound generation, most take the attitude *bah, my smart phone has a pedometer and heart monitor, I'm upright and moving, I be fine.*

Public schools in the west today are littered with the consequences of the previous chapter's discussion. This is a generation who have for role models the Kardashians, Kanye West, Miley Cyrus or George Clooney. Ask almost any teenager who won the Civil War and answers will range from "We did?" to "Uh, I don't know" and all points in between. But ask them who stars on <u>Twilight</u> and the answer comes quick as greased lightning. They learn sex education in the locker room, like many previous generations, but with the added dubious benefit of a Public School system determined to remove as much parental influence as possible, creating loyal servants of the State, incapable of thinking for themselves and with no guidance on how to control natural passions.

Sex education begins as young as five years old with rules on white privilege, gender neutrality, or here's a new term in vogue in progressive circles to add to our English vocabulary "gender fluidity". Yeah, that's the ticket. Today you can feel like a woman and voila! You're a woman! Tomorrow, maybe you feel like a man. So be it and so it is. What's next? You feel like an alligator so you eat people?

Boys whose only mentors are shallow Hollywood personalities grow up emulating those they look up to. Lyrics in today's music spew anti-social programming, disrespect for law and order, hatred of anything moral and good. Computer games are filled with violence, death and every latent undesirable human trait that civilized society has sought to minimize for six thousand years. The obvious reason in this writer's opinion is a suffocating lack of sound Biblical teaching in the home and in the school.

We have a medical paradigm that floods our living rooms and our minds with television programming advertising a huge and growing list of pharmaceuticals that come with a laundry list of dangerous side-effects. (Hint: they are not "side-effects. They are the effects of the drug on the human body. Any beneficial effect is actually the "side-effect". But ask your Doctor anyway "Is Brand X right for me?")

Many school nurses legally dispense birth control pills to young girls, often without parents' consent or knowledge. Gardasil, a recombinant human papillomavirus vaccine, is recommended and widely dispensed to pre-adolescent children with the foregone assumption that they will have pre-marital sex, thereby creating a self-fulfilling prophecy. If the adults in their lives have already concluded they will give in to peer pressure and engage in premarital sex, then why not? After all, everybody's doing it, right?

Statistically and experientially it is proven that church kids are not immune to the changes in social mores. Our children need something to believe in. They need someone to come to them in their moral confusion, and say *"I believe in you! I believe you can do great things! I believe you can be anything you want to be. You have wings to soar. I believe you can fly! You don't have to follow the crowd. You can grow to adulthood with your morals intact. Be a leader for your generation! You are beautiful in modesty. You don't have to dress to attract. The purity of your modesty will draw the right people to you. As a girl, you were endowed at creation with dignity and a purpose. As a boy, you have within you the capacity to become a prophet, priest and king in your own home, to the nation and to the world. Defend your destiny at all costs!"*

It was much different for children growing up in Galilee. Most people lived in small villages, some with as few as fifty to a hundred people. Boys and girls experienced a number of rites of passage in their lives, culminating in a bar or bat mitzvah, son or daughter of the Commandment. It meant they were of an age to be personally responsible to the God of Abraham, Isaac and Jacob. Like children today, the attended school and learned the three R's (readin', writin' and 'rithmetic) the way we once did in America

In the Dust of the Rabbi

Come. Let's take a trip. Come with me to once upon a time, to a place not so far away, a trip across time and space, to an area along the northern coast of the Sea of Galilee in first century Israel. Often called the triangle, it was an area spotted with small villages whose Israelite inhabitants were passionate about family, passionate about community, passionate about their ancient traditions. They were a people with a passionate commitment to Torah.

Narrow your focus and zoom in on one specific fishing village, tiny by today's standards. Not unlike a dozen similar villages in the area, the little town of Bethsaida pulses with activity. Breathe deep the plethora of odors, the pungent sea smells of the waters nearby, an ocean teeming with life.

Walk along one of the streets, actually no more than a mere footpath between buildings, as your eyes water from acrid smoke billowing from a number of chimneys. Inhale the enticing scent of baking bread, the satisfying aroma of spices and herbs used in recipes passed down from generations.

Observe the battered fishing boats of simple fishermen, plying their trades just as their fathers did and their fathers before them. Listen to the cacophony of sounds assaulting your ears, of the carpenter as he lovingly crafts his woodwork, or the lively debate around the table in the synagogue as Rabbis from the area discuss the nuances of and proper interpretation of Holy Writ.

The clamor of children running and playing is not unlike the sounds of childhood from any age. Listen carefully and you'll hear the names of some of the boys at play as they call to each other in their youthful exuberance.

Peter. "Hey guys! Let's go play some b-ball"

James. "Sounds good. I'll go get John and meet you at the ball park."

John. "I'm game. Let's go! Anybody seen Phillip?"

Andrew. "Nope. He's disappeared again."

Well, maybe not exactly like that. But you get my drift.

These five grew up like every other boy in that culture. They played together. They worshiped together. They went to school together.

They have one distinction that differentiates them from others. Of the twelve men Jesus chose to be His disciples, these five all came from this tiny fishing village, Bethsaida, and all five of them had gone on to carry on their respective family vocations, having failed to rise beyond their basic Torah studies.

Bet Sefer

PAGE 66 TOP — FAILED IN THE EYES OF THE RELIGIOUS SYSTEM THEN

For Jews living in Jesus' day, there were three separate educational venues. The first was called *Bet Sefer*, Hebrew for *house of the book*.

At the tender age of six Jewish children began their formal education, attending until the age of twelve. Both boys and girls attended synagogue school and learned to read and write. The textbook was a Torah scroll and the goal was not just to read but to *memorize* the sacred text. Can you imagine?

As a child of six, you would go to the synagogue and the most respected man in the city would greet you with a slate and he would put a dollop of honey on the slate and then he would remove the ancient scroll of the Torah. As you sat speechless and in awe, the rabbi would have you taste the honey on your slate and tell you that the Torah is sweeter than the honeycomb.[47]

Can you imagine the impact this would have on a young child? You can bet that whenever that child tasted honey he was always reminded of the Word of God! Now at the conclusion of this period of schooling, a bar mitzvah for the boy welcomed him into the community as a full-fledged male member. Following this sacred milestone, usually the boy then began to learn the family trade. From this point, only the best of the best continued in their education. — *OTHERS "FAILED" OF SORTS*

Bet Midrash

For the best of the best, the next educational opportunity was called *Bet Midrash*. Boys - from age 13 to 15 - who were deemed worthy to continue their educational pursuits went on to study (and memorize) the entire Tanach, - the Old Testament as many modern believers would call it - as well as learning the family trade. (It is noteworthy that few, if any, of Jesus's disciples made it this far in their educational training.) Very few were selected for this pursuit.

Bet Talmud

Of those who finished *Bet Midrash*, again only the best of the best were able to pursue the final educational leg, which was called *Bet Talmud*. This was the longest in duration; it went from the age of 15 to 30. Following custom,

---

[47] Psa 19:10 More to be desired are they than gold, yea, than much fine gold: sweeter also than honey and the honeycomb.

they went to Capernaum, where noted Rabbis gathered to teach and discuss Torah.

The one desiring to advance to this level followed a pattern, approaching the Rabbi of his choice and asking him point blank, *"may I follow you?"* Few were chosen. Most were rejected after the Rabbi observed him in his daily habits, discerning and judging his character to determine if the candidate truly had the motivation and gifting that fit the vocation. Most were told *"Go. Learn your father's trade. Learn Torah in the synagogue with your brethren."*

To participate, he must be invited by a Rabbi and, if selected, he would begin a process of grooming that would lead to the potential of becoming a Rabbi at age thirty. Those who were chosen were referred to as *talmidim,* meaning *students* or *learners.* They would literally follow in the dust of their rabbi, desiring to emulate him in all of his mannerisms. They would eat the same food in exactly the same way as their rabbi. They would go to sleep and awaken the same way as their rabbi and, more importantly, they would learn to study Torah and understand God the *exact* same way as their Rabbi. Having reached a sufficient level of development in Torah understanding, wisdom and ability to communicate under the Rabbi's tutelage, the disciple is told *"Go. Continue your Torah studies in synagogue. Give feet to your faith in God and walk according to the way, the truth and the life* (a euphemism for Torah). *Go and make disciples of your own."*

Walk This Way → THUS THE RISK OF FOLLOWING MAN VS GOD.

It was the ultimate *"Walk this way"* relationship. I'm reminded of the character Igor played by Marty Feldman in the Mel Brooks movie, <u>Young Frankenstein,</u> pronounced *Fronkensteen*. If you remember the movie, you'll recall Igor had a migrating hump on his back and walked seriously slumped over with a lumbering gait. Leading Gene Wilder's character down a set of stairs he says *"walk this way"*. Wilder, confused but obedient, slouched over and in classic vaudeville style followed him in like manner. Would that we as Christians were as attentive in following Jesus as He walked!

Peter, James, John, Andrew and Philip had gone as far as they could with their formal schooling. They were well versed in the teachings of the Torah. But they recognized that their calling was not as a Rabbi and were content to follow in their earthly Fathers' footsteps in the family trade. What Jesus did was <u>a stunning departure from tradition</u>. <u>The supreme Rabbi of Rabbis sought and called any and all from every walk of life to be his disciples</u>

rather than letting them seek Him out. They didn't choose Him. He chose them!

We see a type of this process in I Kings 19:16[48]. Most translations say *"in your room"* in the verse. The Hebrew word is tachat, meaning in lieu of or take the place of. The prophet Elijah is instructed to find and anoint Elisha to be his successor as prophet of YHWH. We see in this event a further type or shadow of Messiah telling his disciples that upon his departure from earth, they would be his replacement as the light of the world.

Choices – Leaving and Entering

All of life is an unending chain of choices, a process of leaving and entering. We leave the womb to enter life in this world. We leave childhood to enter into adulthood. We leave single life to enter into marriage. We leave school to enter the workplace.

We make decisions every waking moment about all manner of choices such as which school to attend, who to marry, or which car to buy along with a dizzying array of alternatives we're continually faced with on a day to day basis.

The most important leaving and entering one ever does in life is to leave the old life of sin and enter into new life of faith in the Savior. When we are born again, we become a new creature in Christ. We literally become something or someone that never existed before. We are challenged thereafter throughout our walk in this earthly life with the challenge to *"come out of her my people"*[49].

People are free to choose belief in the insidious lie of the Universal Fatherhood of God/Universal Brotherhood of man, that all will be saved regardless of personal belief and behavior. Or one may accept Biblical truth that all have sinned and come short of the glory of God and are in desperate need of a Savior. You're either a child of God or you're not. God will be Savior or Judge. The choice is yours.

---

[48] 1Ki 19:16 And Jehu the son of Nimshi shalt thou anoint to be king over Israel: and Elisha the son of Shaphat of Abelmeholah shalt thou anoint to be prophet in thy room.

[49] Rev 18:4 And I heard another voice from heaven, saying, Come out of her, my people, that ye be not partakers of her sins, and that ye receive not of her plagues.

The beauty, the awe-inspiring truth, is that He went to those who failed in spiritual attainment, who were not considered good enough to measure up to the exalted expectations of the religious leadership and said "*Come. Follow Me*". I choose **you**. I believe in **you**. Here is the magnificent One, the King of all Kings, who came to them in their failures and inadequacies and He says to the five from Bethsaida, to the others in His circle of disciples and extended family, to those who have failed in the eyes of the religious system, to you and me He says "**I believe in you**! Come. Follow me."

I may have decided to follow Jesus, but there is more to being a disciple than a hastily repeated prayer at the end of short walk down the aisle. A disciple is one that Jesus chooses to follow Him. The Bible is replete with words such as *"chosen", "elect", "predestined"* and the like. Once chosen, the true disciple devotes his or her life to following in the footsteps of the Messiah, walking, behaving, believing like the Master, Rabbi Yeshua. He demands we take up our cross and follow Him; that we love Him above and beyond anything or anyone else. Anything less and He says one is not worthy to be His disciple.

A poignant example of the impossible becoming possible occurred one day on the stormy Sea of Galilee. Peter saw Jesus walking on the water and said *"if that's you, bid me come"* and Jesus called him. In essence Jesus was saying to Peter *"If you will trust me, I believe in you! I believe you can walk on water if you'll believe with me."* Peter wavered in his belief that Jesus believed in him, trusting his physical senses and the impossibility of what was going on, and he sank. Many of us like to berate Peter for his unbelief. After all, here he was in the divine presence, actually walking on water yet still he doubted. But, dear prideful ones, **Peter stepped out of the boat!** How many of us have demonstrated a tiny fraction of that level of faith and stepped out our boats? Faith can move a mountain. Faith can calm the stormy sea. Faith can change the person and the world he lives in, **but you have to step out of the boat!** If Jesus believes in you, then start to believe in yourself. It'll change your life forever. *POWER ONLY FLOWS WHEN RELEASED + DIRECTED*

In the Footsteps of Messiah

It appears that Jesus Himself followed this model. At twelve we know that He attended Passover in Jerusalem. He began His formal ministry at age thirty. The Bible is silent as far as His mentors, although there is evidence He followed established rules of interpretation passed down through generations from the time of Ezra and Nehemiah. We do know that He selected His disciples and, just like those young fifteen year olds when

IF HE WAS A FATHER + PROVIDER IN HIS FATHER'S ABSENCE HE WOULD HAVE BEEN TREATED AS AN OLDER MAN PERHAPS.

invited to *Bet Talmud*, they left everything to follow after this Rabbi from Galilee. No doubt they walked in His dust, wanting to be just like their Rabbi. They were His *talmidim* or learners, students. History and the written Word reveal to us that Jesus trained His *talmidim* in three years, not fifteen and His training was so inspired that they, His *talmidim*, literally changed the world.

OR A FEW MONTHS

Now, back to the beginning. How are we as the Church doing in raising up *talmidim*? How is the church doing in making disciples of Christ? Are we producing disciples who are duplicates of Jesus, who are walking as he walked and behaving as he behaved, or are we making copies of ourselves, Christians who look nothing like the Savior we claim to follow, lawbreakers and traditionalists made in the image of the Church Fathers?

I believe the time has come to reclaim discipleship and to again raise the bar. We all need to follow in the dust of our Rabbi. But where do we start? We start in the same place as those six year old children in Galillee - we start with the Word of God.

TODD'S PATH FOR OTHERS:
PS 119
PR 1-8
GEN - DEUT
JOHN
ACTS
PETER
JAMES
1-3 JOHN
ROMANS
1-2 COR
COL
GAL
HEB

A FOUNDATION IN TRUTH NEED GO TO COMPREHEND NEW FACTS

6
THE GREAT DIVIDE

Two Kinds of People

Religion statistics expert George **Barna** says America is headed for *"310 million people with 310 million religions."*[50] While that is obviously an extreme exaggeration, he makes a valid point.

Estimates vary, but the general consensus is that there are somewhere between 34,000 and 41,000 Christian denominations, give or take a few thousand. That's an awful lot of churches for an institution that claims to have as its foundation the same Bible which says there is only one Body[51]. That same Bible says the world, that is, unbelievers, will know we are Jesus' disciples[52] based on how we display love for one another.

Humanity is a complex matrix of dissimilar personalities and a bewildering array of contradictory behaviors. People are diverse and multifaceted creatures, but many differences between us can nonetheless be boiled down into a simple, binary distinction.

---

[50] USA Today, Sep 12, 2011

[51] Eph. **Eph 4:4-6** *There is* one body, and one Spirit, even as ye are called in one hope of your calling; One Lord, one faith, one baptism, One God and Father of all, who *is* above all, and through all, and in you all.

[52] **Joh 13:35** By this shall all *men* know that ye are my disciples, if ye have love one to another.

Sometimes, let's be honest, you can divide the whole world down to just two kinds of people. Like these quotes: (attribution is given to those whose authorship is known. The others are assumed to be in public domain.)

"There are two kinds of people in the world, those who believe there are two kinds of people in the world and those who don't." [53]

There are three kinds of people in the world: Those who know math and those who don't.

"There are two kinds of people in the world, those with loaded guns, and those who dig. You dig." [54]

There are two kinds of people in the world: Me and You.

"For my grandfather, there were two kinds of people in the world: Those who agreed with him, and those who hadn't yet agreed with him." [55]

And my favorite:

There are two kinds of people: those who can extrapolate from incomplete data.

Levity aside, there really are only two kinds of people in the world according to the Bible. Jesus made a clear distinction between two groups of people.[56]

In the world of man, there are no fence sitters on the question of eternal destiny. One is free to accept God's offer of eternal life or equally free to reject it. In Biblical terminology, one is either saved or one is not saved; born again or not. One's name is written in the Book of Life or it is not. Those who receive Him are given the privilege of being a child of the Most High.[57] One is saved by grace through faith[58] or faces the alternative, an

---

[53] Robert Benchley's *Law of Distinction*

[54] Clint Eastwood, 1966, "The Good, The Bad and The Ugly"

[55] *B. Spira*

[56] **Luk 11:23** He that is not with me is against me: and he that gathereth not with me scattereth.

[57] **Joh 1:12** But as many as received him, to them gave he power to become the sons of God, *even* to them that believe on his name:

[58] Eph. 2:8,9

eternal separation from the Presence of God.[59]

The question must be asked: how did the **one body** come to be so fractured? Why is there such a great divide in the Body of Christ? Not only is the Church divided into a patchwork of denominational creeds and distinctions, but we find ourselves totally alienated from early church understanding and interpretation of Scripture. If Jesus was Jewish, and **all** of His early disciples were Jewish, and every passage in the New Testament was written by Jews with a Jewish cultural background and a Hebraic worldview, with Torah as their foundation, how and why did the Church stray so far from her Biblical roots? ↓ BECOME ANTI-JEWISH / SEMETIC

If 1st century Christians walked into most church services today, I daresay they wouldn't recognize it. They would have no idea they were with people who worshiped the same Yeshua they worshiped.

The early Church kept the seventh day Sabbath, celebrated the Leviticus 23 feasts, followed in the footsteps of the Master and emulated everything He said and did and taught others to do the same. How does the modern Church find herself so far removed from those early worship practices? Let us together try to Biblically, historically and accurately answer those questions as we progress.

A Big Tent

It takes very little research to find that much of modern Christianity's sacraments and holiday celebrations are based on ancient pagan worship practices introduced early in the life of the Church. These traditions were incorporated into Christian practice by a decidedly anti-Semitic gentile segment, given authority by the increasingly influential Catholic Church and codified by Emperor Constantine in 325 A.D.

Mixture of things profane with holy has always been a big deal with the Father. Whether weaving cloth with a mixture of animal and plant fiber, or of mixing the holy things of Christ with the things of Belial, mixture is anathema in the eyes of God. There has been a fusion of lies mixed truth within the faith for centuries. Through the edicts of Constantine, paganism

---

[59] Isa 59:2 But your iniquities have separated between you and your God, and your sins have hid his face from you, that he will not hear.

and Christianity joined hands to become the ultimate state-sanctioned church known as the Holy Roman Empire.

In the ultimate big tent revival, Constantine opened the floodgates of the pasture to the tares, those who served to promote stability within his empire but diluted almost beyond recognition the pure message of Biblical faith. Constantine, a brilliant strategist, realized the surest way to unite his kingdom and bring harmony in his kingdom was to blend Christianity with the many and varied cultural expressions of sun worship. The Church of Rome was complicit in this undertaking and successfully passed on for the next eighteen hundred years the travesty of a hybrid Gospel.

The bishops at Rome also claimed Peter as the head of the church, or the Vicar of Christ. The word vicar is where we get the word vicarious which means in place of or in the stead of. Ephesians 4:15[60] says Jesus is the head of the Church. There is no other head, Catholic or otherwise.

Ironically, the Peter buried underneath St. Peter's Basilica on the grounds of the Vatican was likely Simon Magus, the sorcerer, the same one that Simon Peter contended with in the book of Acts.[61] Developing a non-biblical doctrine of "apostolic succession," the bishops claimed that the authority conferred on Peter was transferred to succeeding popes. The "Saint Peter" that was created was actually a combination of pagan idolatry and Christian veneration. Even today, the statue in St. Peter's Cathedral in Rome includes a solar disk above his head. Tradition has it that this was actually a statue of Jupiter taken from a pagan temple and simply renamed "St. Peter". Sun worship, which is practiced by virtually every pagan religion in the world, began appearing in Christian art. The halos often seen on Christ and Mary are actually ancient symbols of sun worship. Pictures of Madonna (Mary) was depicted holding sun disks.

One of the earliest entrances of sun worship into the church was through the spring pagan festival. The festival honored the goddess Ishtar, and one of the more popular tales of this time concerned the god Attis, who was said to be resurrected each year during the month of March. According to

---

60 Eph 4:15 But speaking the truth in love, may grow up into him in all things, which is the head, even Christ:

61 Act 8:9 But there was a certain man, called Simon, which beforetime in the same city used sorcery, and bewitched the people of Samaria, giving out that himself was some great one:

one tradition, the festival of Attis began as a day of blood on a black Friday and culminated after three days in a day of rejoicing over a resurrection. These spring festivals eventually became the Christian festival of Easter, complete with eggs and rabbits, both ancient pagan symbols of fertility. All of this is easily shown to be sourced from the Tower of Babel, Nimrod, his wife Semiramis and Tammuz. The origin of the practice of coloring Easter eggs dates from the horrific ritual of sacrificing a child born of one of the vestal virgins impregnated on the previous winter solstice on the altar, after which the blood is captured in a chalice and used to paint the eggs, a symbol of the fertility of the goddess Ishtar.

At the Council of Nicaea in 325 A.D., Constantine also persuaded those in attendance that only one Easter "Resurrection" day should be kept. *"Our Savior has left us only one festal day ... and he desired to establish only one Catholic Church,"* he argued. Then he added this significant statement. *"You should consider ... that we should have nothing in common with the Jews."*

Constantine felt that the Jews were murderers of the Lord, and therefore desired to blot out any links between Christianity and Judaism. In persuading the Christian church to drop the ancient biblical Sabbath, given at Creation, and replacing it with Sunday worship, the schism between Christianity and its Jewish roots was firmly established as Church doctrine that carried right through the Reformation into Protestant practice today.

"The Church made a sacred day of Sunday largely because it was the weekly festival of the sun; for it was a definite Christian policy to take over the pagan festivals endeared to the people by tradition, and to give them a Christian significance." Pope Sylvester I (314–335)

In decreeing that *"the rest of the Sabbath should be transferred to the Lord's day"* Constantine made Christian Sunday keeping official. With an incredible sleight of hand the Devil sneaked sun worship into Christianity by exchanging the true Christian day of worship for the day dedicated to ancient sun worship.

No matter how we may justify keeping un-Biblical worship practices by "Christianizing" them, God's Word on the matter never changes. When God said *"don't worship me the same way the pagans worship their false gods"*[62], He

---

[62] **Deu 12:30** Take heed to thyself that thou be not snared by following them, after that they be destroyed from before thee; and that thou enquire not after their gods, saying, How did these nations serve their gods? even so will I do

meant **don't worship Him in the same way the pagans worship their false gods!**

A common defense of many Christians who are sincere in their justification of celebrations that are clearly of pagan origin goes something like this *"That's not what it means to me"* or *"God knows my heart"*. Well, dear heart that is exactly the problem. God does know our hearts and he says it is desperately wicked.[63] And frankly, it really doesn't matter what something means to me. What matters, the only thing that matters, is what does it mean to the Father? Anything beyond that is compromise.

The sin of the golden calf at Mt. Sinai is a clear demonstration of God's displeasure with approaching Him through pagan worship practice. While Moses was forty days on the mountain, the people became fearful, wondering if Moses's absence meant he had died while in the presence of God who they were called to follow. Look carefully at what the Scripture says:

> Exo 32:5,6 *"And when Aaron saw it, he built an altar before it; and Aaron made proclamation, and said, Tomorrow is a feast to YHWH." And they rose up early on the morrow, and offered burnt offerings, and brought peace offerings; and the people sat down to eat and to drink, and rose up to play."*

Note carefully that they did all this in honor of the true God, YHWH. There must have been many who said to Moses after he came down from the mountain top *"That's not what it means to me. God knows my heart."* God obviously rejected that defense then and He rejects it now. One might be inclined to counter with "how can the majority be wrong? Surely the vast majority of Christians throughout history is proof that God ordained it this way." My answer is since when is the majority proof of anything? Too often

---

likewise.

Deu 12:31 Thou shalt not do so unto the LORD thy God: for every abomination to the LORD, which he hateth, have they done unto their gods; for even their sons and their daughters they have burnt in the fire to their gods.

Deu 12:32 What thing soever I command you, observe to do it: thou shalt not add thereto, nor diminish from it.

[63] Jer 17:9 The heart is deceitful above all things, and desperately wicked: who can know it?

following the majority means you're going in the wrong direction.

Whence the Original Christians?

Never satisfied with going quietly into the night, man is master of division. We split the atom, we can by golly split the church! God takes two and makes them one. We humans seem to delight at turning one into two. We separate husband from wife in divorce. We separate church and state with laws that relegate faith to the home and out of public view. We separate futurists from historicists, Baptists from Pentecostals, Presbyterians from Lutherans. We separate the One New Man into a false narrative of two distinct people groups called "Jews and Christians".

I am not advocating an ecumenical kumbaya. What I am encouraging is a restoration of the church as it was instituted in the first century. How do we do that? We go back; back to the beginning, back to observe and emulate how the Church functioned in the beginning.

There will be the temptation to read into this - remember eisigesis, imparting a preconceived belief into the text - and insist the writer is saying *we must all be Jews now*. Nothing could be further from the truth. We gentiles are recipients of the amazing gift of salvation by grace thanks to the Jews[64], but genetically we are the offspring of our gentile ancestors and will never become somehow mystically transformed into Jews with a Jewish bloodline. However, we are grafted[65] into a Jewish Messiah who was Hebrew in thought, nature, custom and worship practice.

What happened to the original Messianic Jews, the Jewish Christians, and the gentile believers who followed the Messiah as they were taught by those Torah observant Jewish believers? They were key figures in early Christianity, perhaps even with a divine mandate. But those who believed in

---

[64] Joh 4:22 You worship what you do not know; we worship what we know, for salvation is from the Jews.
[65] Rom 11:17-18 And if some of the branches be broken off, and thou, being a wild olive tree, wert graffed in among them, and with them partakest of the root and fatness of the olive tree; Boast not against the branches. But if thou boast, thou bearest not the root, but the root thee.

Jesus while also following the whole Torah grew apart from both mainstream Jews and Gentile Christians.

Dam Lies

In the 4th Century, as Rome was becoming officially Christian by decree, Christianity divested itself of many elements of Jewish theology and worship, and declared such sects heretical.

It was during this time that a clear separation of God's Word into two distinct sections became the predominant understanding of the Hebrew Scriptures and the Apostolic writings, radically affecting Christian theological thought and interpretation of Holy Writ. A new paradigm developed that separated the *"testaments"*, the old being replaced by the new. The mental connection is made that the old is good but the new is better.

Born and raised at the foot of the Rocky Mountains, I have been many times to the top of the Continental Divide. Water flows East or West from the summit depending on which side of the divide they are. Like the mountain range that divides the continent, a spiritual Great Divide was created that profoundly influenced Christian thought, separating God's Holy Word into two separate and distinct religious concepts.

That dam is the page in your Bible that says, "The New Testament." But it's more than a page; it's really a mind-set that this page represents. It's a false demarcation implying a radical separation between the Old Testament and the New Testament. This way of thinking dams up the waters of the first part of the Bible from the last part of the Bible. Christians are taught there are two distinct, often even opposing bodies of water. They look to the left and see the river of law in the OT; look to the right and they see the river of grace in the NT.

They see a lifeless body of bitter waters in the Old Testament that makes demands on how we should live a righteous life with no means to do so. In the New Testament they see a river of living water that flows from a source separate and distinct from the Old.

Ripping the page out of the Bible that divorces the Old Testament from the New may symbolically restore them to their rightful unity. Ripping that mindset from the collective mind of Christianity is a task only the Father will accomplish. We as Christians heard there are prophecies of the Messiah in the Old Testament; that at least Psalm 22 and Isaiah 53 tell us about the suffering servant; that the Savior would be born of a virgin and other prophetic signs as proof of His divine appearance. But by and large, for most, the Old Testament remains a Christless book, a book full of law and void of grace.

Getting Christ Out Of Christmas

The hue and cry is heard every year beginning in the fall to *put Christ back in Christmas*.

Folks, Jesus never was in Christmas! Some argue *"I don't offer children to the fires of Molech"*. Really? That's your argument? You don't go to the horrific extreme of burning your children in sacrifice, therefore you are justified doing the other parts and that makes it okay? That's a bit like saying well, I may have lustful thoughts, but at least I don't commit adultery. Hmmm …?

This may be the first and only time many will read the truth about our Christianized paganism. Stay with me. If I'm wrong, no harm no foul. But if I'm right, you don't want to be on the wrong side of this and find yourself fighting against God.[66] So for those who can't be bothered with proving these allegations, let us do a quick summary of the elements of Christmas in their original context.

Every year, people all over the world, believers and atheists alike, celebrate Christmas, with all its commercial over-buying and frenetic activity. Christians everywhere – at least those in western countries – will have knelt before their Christmas trees, opened all their myriad gifts, many of which will be promptly returned to their retail sources, and stuffed themselves with hearty helpings of ham, dressing, pie and sundry other fattening culinary fare.

Many will have watched Kirk Cameron's Saving Christmas, released in

---

[66] **Act 5:38** And now I say unto you, Refrain from these men, and let them alone: for if this counsel or this work be of men, it will come to nought:
Act 5:39 But if it be of God, ye cannot overthrow it; lest haply ye be found even to fight against God.

2014, relieved that someone with visibility and influence comes to the rescue of Christianity's most sacred holidays. However, it becomes readily evident that his purpose in producing the film was not to rescue Christmas from the pagans and atheists. No, it was clearly a response to the growing number of Christians who have in recent years opted to ditch worship practices rooted in paganism in favor of Bible based celebrations. The film is his attempt to bring them back *"into the fold"*. His fallacious, ludicrous argument was that pagans stole it from Christians and we needed to take it back. Talk about revisionism! Five minutes on Google would provide ample documentation of the roots of Christmas and Easter.

There's a spiritual reason for the growing number of Christians who are turning away from traditional celebrations that are demonstrably rooted in paganism, "Christianized" by the Catholic church, and maintained in the Protestant churches at the time of the Reformation. The Protestant Church et al, rightfully rejected the claims of Papal authority with its Mary worship, indulgences and multitude of doctrinal perversions, without debate pagan at their roots, while retaining many aspects of cultic worship practices introduced into the Catholic Church at its inception.

Voices will have rung out in joyful harmony, singing that beautiful hymn "O Holy Night", rejoicing over the night of "our dear Savior's birth". Never mind the well-known fact that December 25th was not the day of our Savior's birth, but was indeed a celebration that dates all the way back to the tower of Babel. For now, I have a number of questions for my Christian friends, questions that will anger some. Some will be offended, close the book and not read another word. But they are questions that Christians must answer honestly if we are true to the claim of being faithful students of God's Word.

Christians would be mortified if someone suggested we take a golden calf and Christianize it by saying the gold speaks of Jesus' deity, and the bull represents His strength and authority, which by the way is precisely what the ancient script portrays. No. One would be tarred and feathered; run out of town on a rail; called a blasphemer and a heretic. Yet when confronted with the truth of the roots of Christmas, the symbolism that was blatantly adopted and Christianized, Christians are horrified and offer a kneejerk response with justifications like the green tree represents His eternal life, gold His deity, silver redemption, red His blood, and on and on.

Mystery Babylon

We are told multiple times to come out of Mystery Babylon, to separate ourselves from the ways of the world; to be holy even as He is holy. We're told that to be friends of the world is to be an enemy of Christ.

You agree that Jesus was probably not born on December 25th but you celebrate his birth on that day anyway. Why?

You admit the trappings have pagan beginnings, but you do it anyway. Why?

You admit the tree has nothing to do with the birth of Jesus, but you kneel before it once a year on Christmas morning anyway. Why?

Paul is un-ambiguous in his entreaty[67] to those who would call themselves sons and daughters of the Most High. Have nothing, NOTHING to do with the deeds of darkness. We quote this verse about coming out, but we stay in. Why?

We lament the drastic decline of morals and lawlessness in this country without once questioning lawlessness in the Church.

This is going to annoy many, maybe alienate some. But these are the facts of the roots of Christmas celebration. I hope the Spirit uses it to shake you to the core. The tree was symbolic of a reincarnated Tammuz. It represented the penis of god while the wreath was symbolic of the vagina of

---

[67] 2Co 6:14 Be ye not unequally yoked together with unbelievers: for what fellowship hath righteousness with unrighteousness? and what communion hath light with darkness?
2Co 6:15 And what concord hath Christ with Belial? or what part hath he that believeth with an infidel?
2Co 6:16 And what agreement hath the temple of God with idols? for ye are the temple of the living God; as God hath said, I will dwell in them, and walk in them; and I will be their God, and they shall be my people.
2Co 6:17 Wherefore come out from among them, and be ye separate, saith the Lord, and touch not the unclean thing; and I will receive you,
2Co 6:18 And will be a Father unto you, and ye shall be my sons and daughters, saith the Lord Almighty.

the queen of heaven, also called the mother of god. Tinsel represented the sperm of god, while a bonfire, the burning of a yule log, pictured his death and reincarnation. This is just the tip of the iceberg. Anyone wishing to seriously come all the way out of Babylon will find a plethora of information about the satanic roots of Christianity's two major holidays.

Many will say *"I'm not worshiping false gods"*. Nobody says you are. What you are doing though is worshiping the true God in ways that He commanded His people NOT TO DO!

It stands to reason that if we're going to publicly ask the question *"What would Jesus do?"* we ought to be honest and admit we're really not doing what He did. Once we know what He did, aren't we then responsible to **do what He did?** Sadly, experience shows that what we do instead is misapply Paul's writing and make him to be superior to Jesus, teaching the Church to disobey Christ's clear teaching.

A particular teaching that is prevalent in most of main stream Christianity is one whose beginnings can be traced to a specific time frame and specific teachers in American Christian development. It is a teaching that arguably has done the greatest damage to the idea of covenant established in the Old Testament and adhered to right up until the mid-1800s. That teaching is the idea that the Church supplanted Israel and is now by the grace of God the true *"spiritual Israel"*, which gave rise to two distorted views of Scriptural hermeneutics that have shaped the fundamental doctrines of the Church for over a hundred and fifty years.

Interpreting Hebrew text with a Western/Christian mindset out of context forces other passages to be interpreted in a way that supports that interpretation. For example, if Israel is rejected, then the Church is the recipient of the New Covenant, ergo the Church is Spiritual Israel. Never mind that the Scripture clearly says the Covenant was made with Israel and ONLY with Israel. Friends, if we have to spiritualize any part of Scripture in order to make it fit our current understanding, our understanding must be questioned. We've heard it said a thousand times: God said what He means and means what He says. It's high time we live what we say we believe.

7
REPLACEMENT THEOLOGY

Barna Research Group's findings from 2009 contained the following quote: *"The problem facing the Christian church is not that people lack a complete set of beliefs; the problem is that they have a full slate of beliefs in mind, which they think are consistent with biblical teachings, and they are neither open to being proven wrong nor to learning new insights."*

The War on Truth

"Each of us tends to think we see things as they are, that we are objective. But this is not the case. We see the world, not as it is, but as we are - or as we are conditioned to see it". - Stephen. R. Covey

"We do not see things as they are. We see things as we are."— Rabbi Shemuel ben Nachmani, as quoted in the Talmudic tractate Berakhot (55b.)

1891 an instructor of elocution at Harvard College published a textbook about oratory which included the following:

*"It has been well said that **we do not see things as they are, but as we are ourselves.** Every man looks through the eyes of his prejudices, of his preconceived notions. Hence, it is the most difficult thing in the world to broaden a man so that he will realize truth as other men see it."*

In 1914 a newspaper column presenting homilies contained an instance of the expression:

"As a man thinketh in his heart, so is he. As a man sees in his heart, so he sees. Through unclean windows, lenses, senses, **we see things not as they are but as we are.***"*

It is said truth is the first casualty of war.

Since the beginning of time, war has been waged against the Seed of the woman and all those who believe in Him. The adversary's ceaseless goal has always been to rid the world of believers and those who profess Jesus as their one true Lord and Savior. Satan's most effective ploy has been to call into question the veracity of God's Word with the challenge *"hath God said?"* Did God really mean Adam and Eve were forbidden from eating the fruit of a particular tree, or was that simply a story we view to be spiritualized, leaving it open to human interpretation and personalized however we understand it? Was the seminal event in the Garden simply meant as allegory, something from which we should glean spiritual understanding but otherwise relegate to the dustbin of personal interpretation, or was there a literal tree with literal fruit which God literally forbade Adam and Eve to ingest?

Satan asks the same question today: Hath God really said? Did God really mean His Word is eternal, or did He mean it is subject to change based on interpretations handed down from Church fathers of antiquity? Did God really do away with His Torah, hanging it on the cross with Jesus at the crucifixion? Did He really cancel His Feasts and replace them with un-Biblical holidays, or change the seventh day Sabbath to Sunday and a multitude of other precepts that the church today insists were intended for another people in another time?

Did the chosen people forfeit their place in covenant relationship due to their failure to live up to the expectations of a demanding God? The answers to these questions go right to the heart of the cosmic battle that rages between the devil and mankind: Does the eternal God make promises only to change them at a later time? If He could do that, make promises to the Jews, only to renege and give those to another group, couldn't He just as easily decide to take back the promises made to the Church?

Has The Church Replaced Israel?

Is there really any role for Israel in God's plan at the end of the age?

For almost two thousand years the Church at large, both Catholic and Protestant, has maintained that due to the Jews' rejection of Jesus as their Messiah, God poured out His wrath on them in 70 A.D., destroying their nation and their temple. Common perception among most church folks is that He washed His hands of them, leaving them with no purpose whatsoever as a nation. In short, because of their rebellion against God in rejecting their Messiah, God replaced Israel with the Church, transferring the blessings originally promised to Israel to the Church. The result of this replacement mentality is utter confusion for those seeking to reconcile God's eternal promises to Israel with the idea of replacing Israel with the Church.

The majority of professing Christians today accept some version of Replacement Theology in varying degrees. Accordingly, they relegate modern day Israel to be coincident but not primary in God's dealings with the world through the Church. Even when the Church acquiesces to the validity of Israel having a place in the last days, it is only as a resumption of God dealing with the world through the Jews after the Church is removed.

The Origin of Replacement Theology

The roots of Replacement Theology and its fruit of anti-Semitism go back almost to the very beginning of Christianity.

Irrespective of the fact that the early assemblies of believers were comprised of Jewish disciples who followed a Jewish Messiah in a Jewish culture with a Jewish world view speaking the Hebrew language, the Church still managed to sever the organic connection of the Church to her Jewish roots.

The distinctive Jewishness of early Christianity began to fade early on, as the Church began to spread beyond Judea. The Gospel message was embraced by more and more Gentiles who had no interest in maintaining contact with the Church's Jewish roots. Even worse, the new Gentile leaders began to aggressively reject the Jews by vilifying them as "Christ killers", ascribing the worst kind of atrocities to them, expanding the separation between Jew and Gentile, setting in granite what would eventually become Church doctrine.

Appeal to the Church Fathers

We don't have to look far to find the roots of Replacement Theology and its attendant Christian anti-Semitism. Seminaries, Bible Colleges and other institutions of religious academia look to early church theologians, reverentially called the **Church Fathers,** for doctrinal foundation. Any doctrinal truth that might be gleaned is clouded by the abhorrent anti-Jewish rhetoric that finds its way into the thinking and teaching of virtually all of their writing. With this thinking as a doctrinal foundation, is it any wonder the Church is in such confusion about her true identity?

Believers in the early church observed the seven Feasts of the Lord outlined in Leviticus 23. Simply put, they are given for God's people as yearly rehearsals in preparation for the ultimate Festival, His Wedding Feast. They kept the seventh day Sabbath. They kept Passover each year, celebrating what Christians today call *communion*, drinking the cup and eating unleavened bread in remembrance of Him who is our true Passover. They practiced adult baptism according to Scripture for those who came to faith in the Messiah. They acknowledged and emphasized the special relationship between God and His covenant people, Israel.

Why would the Church decide to change the Sabbath from the seventh day to Sunday after over a hundred years of keeping Sabbath?

There is only one real reason and that was to differentiate and separate Christianity from her Hebraic roots. Jews had always and still do observe the seventh day Sabbath. What better way to keep them out of the church and separated from salvation in their Messiah than to change the seventh day Sabbath to Sunday?

It's interesting to note the change from Sabbath to Sunday was decreed as Church doctrine at the Council of Laodicea in 360 A.D. We know from Scripture what the future holds for the Church of Laodicea, right?

The doctrine of replacement theology presumes that the church has replaced Israel; that Christians have replaced the Jews and that God has finished with the Jews because of their unbelief.

Satan's goal in spreading the idea of replacement theology is the very same agenda he's always had, to get rid of the Jews. Destroy Israel and he destroys the eternal covenant promise of redemption given to and through the Jewish people.

Replacement Theology Leads to Replacement Reality

It's very difficult for many today to give up unbiblical traditions. They simply can't believe that they've been so wrong and so deceived all these years. Today, most ministries are centered on self-gratifying, self-motivational principles based on half-truths. The church has given over its historic roots to a fat slob called Santa (Satan?) and the goddess of sex called Ishtar, pronounced *Easter*. The church has taken on the character of ancient Babylon and its leaders turn a deaf ear to the Spirit crying *come out of her my people.*

Christmas and Easter will always be popular because the world and its god created them and the world loves its own. Why are the Feasts of the Lord not accepted by the world? Why is Passover not accepted by the world? Why is there such a concerted effort to reject God's holy days in favor of worldly holidays? The answer is simply this: according to Bible prophecy, a one world religion will rise up in the last days, one that will maintain its own traditions and festivals and reject God's feasts as being irrelevant. The Antichrist will have no problem with people celebrating Christmas and Easter. He will have a problem with those who have a testimony of Jesus Christ and who keep His commandments.

> *"Ephraim has mixed himself among the peoples: Ephraim is a cake unturned. Aliens have devoured his strength, but he does not know it."*
> Hosea 7:8-9

The above verse is the state of the church today. It is **half baked**, lacking Godly strength all the while walking in disobedience and not even knowing it.

Of all the quotes of the Church Fathers that pastors and seminary teachers use to reinforce certain points of their sermons, the following writings are never referred to. They're buried in the dark pages of church history. These comments are all shocking indeed. My aim though is to point out the consistent patterns, all of which come against anything and everything Jewish.

These leaders and church fathers were all responsible for changing the entire church into an organization foreign to the original. Let's remind ourselves what the true original was. It was the early church before the advent of Constantine and the Catholics and eventually the reformers. It was a church of Jews and Gentiles, with a Hebraic character and not one single occult, pagan, Babylonian practice. If one read the following quotes from the Church Fathers without knowing who penned them, a person would assume they were spoken by an officer in Nazi Germany.

Ignatius of Antioch (ca 50-117 AD) *"For if we are still practicing Judaism, we admit that we have not received God's favor...it is wrong to talk about Jesus Christ and live like Jews. For Christianity did not believe in Judaism, but Judaism in Christianity"* -- Epistle to the Magnesians

Justin Martyr (100-106 AD) *"We too, would observe your circumcision of the flesh, your Sabbath days, and in a word, all your festivals, if we were not aware of the reason why they were imposed upon you, namely, because of your sins and the hardness of heart. The custom of circumcising the flesh, handed down from Abraham, was given to you as a distinguishing mark, to set you off from other nations and from us Christians. The purpose of this was that you and only you might suffer the afflictions that are now justly yours; that only your land be desolated, and you cities ruined by fire, that the fruits of you land be eaten by strangers before your very eyes; that not one of you be permitted to enter your city of Jerusalem. Your circumcision of the flesh is the only mark by which you can certainly be distinguished from other men...as I stated before it was by reason of your sins and the sins of your fathers that, among other precepts, God imposed upon you the observence of the sabbath as a mark."* -- Dialogue with Trypho

Irenaeus (ca 130-202 AD) — Declared the Jews were disinherited from the grace of God. -- Against Heresies, Book III, Chapter 21

Tertullian (ca 155-230 AD) — Blamed the Jews for the death of Jesus and argued they had been rejected by God.

Origen of Alexandria (185-254 AD) *"We may thus assert in utter confidence that the Jews will not return to their earlier situation, for they have committed the most abominable of crimes, in forming this conspiracy against the Savior of the human race...hence the city where Jesus suffered was necessarily destroyed, the Jewish nation was driven from its country, and another people was called by God to the blessed election."*

The Council of Elvira (305 AD in Spain) — Prohibited Christians from sharing a meal with a Jew, marrying a Jew, blessing a Jew or observing the Sabbath.

The Council of Nicea (325 AD in Turkey) — Changed the celebration of the Resurrection from the Jewish Feast of First Fruits to Easter in an attempt to disassociate it from Jewish feasts. The Council stated: *"For it is unbecoming beyond measure that on this holiest of festivals we should follow the customs of the Jews. Henceforth let us have nothing in common with this odious people..."*

Eusebius (ca 275-339 AD) — Taught that the promises of Scripture were meant for the Gentiles and the curses were meant for the Jews. He also asserted that the Church was the "true Israel."

John Chrysostom (349-407 AD) — One of the "greatest" of church fathers; known as "The Golden Mouthed." *"The synagogue is worse than a brothel...it is the den of scoundrels and the repair of wild beasts...the temple of demons devoted to idolatrous cults...the refuge of brigands and dabauchees, and the cavern of devils. It is a criminal assembly of Jews...a place of meeting for the assassins of Christ... a house worse than a drinking shop...a den of thieves, a house of ill fame, a dwelling of iniquity, the refuge of devils, a gulf and an abyss of perdition."..."I would say the same things about their souls... As for me, I hate the synagogue...I hate the Jews for the same reason."* The Roots of Christian Anti-Semitism by Malcolm Hay

Jerome (ca 347-420 AD) — Described the Jews as "... *serpents wearing the image of Judas. Their psalms and prayers are the braying of donkeys... They are incapable of understanding Scripture...*"

St. Augustine (354-430 AD) — asserted that the Jews deserved death but were destined to "*… wander the earth to witness the victory of the Church over the synagogue.*"

Peter the Venerable (c. 1092-1156 AD) known as "the meekest of men, a model of Christian charity". "*Yes, you Jews. I say, do I address you; you, who till this very day, deny the Son of God. How long, poor wretches, will ye not believe the truth? Truly I doubt whether a Jew can be really human… I lead out from its den a monstrous animal, and show it as a laughing stock in the amphitheater of the world, in the sight of all the people. I bring thee forward, thou Jew, thou brute beast, in the sight of all men.*" -- The Roots of Christian Anti-Semitism" by Malcolm Hay

Martin Luther – (1483-1546)

"*What then shall we Christians do with this damned, rejected race of Jews? Since they live among us and we know about their lying and blasphemy and cursing, we cannot tolerate them if we do not wish to share in their lies, curses, and blasphemy. In this way we cannot quench the inextinguishable fire of divine rage nor convert the Jews. We must prayerfully and reverentially practice a merciful severity. Perhaps we may save a few from the fire and flames [of hell]. We must not seek vengeance. They are surely being punished a thousand times more than we might wish them. Let me give you my honest advice. First, their synagogues should be set on fire, and whatever does not burn up should be covered or spread over with dirt so that no one may ever be able to see a cinder or stone of it. And this ought to be done for the honor of God and of Christianity in order that God may see that we are Christians, and that we have not wittingly tolerated or approved of such public lying, cursing, and blaspheming of His Son and His Christians. Secondly, their homes should likewise be broken down and destroyed. For they perpetrate the same things there that they do in their synagogues. For this reason they ought to be put under one roof or in a stable, like gypsies, in order that they may realize that they are not masters in our land, as they boast, but miserable captives, as they complain of incessantly before God with bitter wailing. Thirdly, they should be deprived of their prayer-books and Talmuds in which such idolatry, lies, cursing, and blasphemy are taught. Fourthly, their rabbis must be forbidden under threat of death to teach any more. Fifthly, passport and traveling privileges should be absolutely forbidden to the Jews. For they have no business in the rural districts since they are not nobles, nor officials,*" *nor merchants, nor the like. Let them stay at home. If you princes and nobles do not close the road legally to such exploiters, then some troop ought to ride against them, for they will learn from this pamphlet what the Jews are and how to handle them and that they ought not to be protected. You ought not, you cannot protect them, unless in the eyes of God you want to share all their abomination...*

To sum up, dear princes and nobles who have Jews in your domains, if this advice of mine does not suit you, then find a better one so that you and we may all be free of this insufferable devilish burden - the Jews. Let the government deal with them in this respect, as I have suggested. But whether the government acts or not, let everyone at least be guided by his own conscience and form for himself a definition or image of a Jew. When you lay eyes on or think of a Jew you must say to yourself: Alas, that mouth which I there behold has cursed and execrated and maligned every Saturday my dear Lord Jesus Christ, who has redeemed me with his precious blood; in addition, it prayed and pleaded before God that I, my wife and children, and all Christians might be stabbed to death and perish miserably. And he himself would gladly do this if he were able, in order to appropriate our goods...

*Such a desperate, thoroughly evil, poisonous, and devilish lot are these Jews, who for these fourteen hundred years have been and still are our plague, our pestilence, and our misfortune. I have read and heard many stories about the Jews which agree with this judgment of Christ, namely, how they have poisoned wells, made assassinations, kidnapped children, as related before. I have heard that one Jew sent another Jew, and this by means of a Christian, a pot of blood, together with a barrel of wine, in which when drunk empty, a dead Jew was found. There are many other similar stories. For their kidnapping of children they have often been burned at the stake or banished (as we already heard). I am well aware that they deny all of this. However, it all coincides with the judgment of Christ which declares that they are venomous, bitter, vindictive, tricky serpents, assassins, and children of the devil, who sting and work harm stealthily wherever they cannot do it openly. For this reason, I would like to see them where there are no Christians. The Turks and other heathen do not tolerate what we Christians endure from these venomous serpents and young devils...**next to the devil, a Christian has no more bitter and galling foe than a Jew.***

There is no other to whom we accord as many benefactions and from whom we suffer as much as we do from these base children of the devil, this brood of vipers."-- On The Jews and Their Lies [Emphasis mine]

In another treatise Luther wrote:

> *"But your [God's] judgment is right, justus es Dominie. Yes, so shall Jews,*
> *but no one else be punished, who held your word and miracles in contempt*
> *and ridiculed, insulted and damned it for such a long time without*
> *interruption, so that they will not fall, like other humans, heathens and all*
> *the others, into sin and death, not up in Hell, nor in the middle of Hell but*
> *in the pit of Hell, as one cannot fall deeper....*
>
> *Even if they were punished in the most gruesome manner that the streets ran*
> *with their blood, that their dead would be counted, not in the hundred*
> *thousands, but in the millions, as happened under Vespasian in Jerusalem*
> *and for evil under Hadrian, still they must insist on being right even if after*
> *these 1,500 years they were in misery another 1,500 years, still God must be*
> *a liar and they must be correct. In sum, they are the devil's children, damned*
> *to Hell...*
>
> *The Jews too got what they deserved. They had been called and elected to be*
> *God's mouth as Jeremiah says...Open your mouth wide and I will fill it; they*
> *however, kept tightly closed their muzzles, eyes, ears, nose, whole heart and*
> *all senses, so he polluted and squirted them so full that it oozes from them in*
> *all places and devil's filth comes from them.*
>
> *Yes, that tastes good to them, into their hearts, they smack their lips like*
> *swine. That is how they want it. Call more: 'Crucify him, crucify him.'*
> *Scream more: 'His blood come upon us and our children.' (Matthew 27:25)*
> *I mean it came and found you...*
>
> *Perhaps, one of the merciful Saints among us Christians may think I am*
> *behaving too crude and disdainfully against the poor, miserable Jews in that I*
> *deal with them so sarcastically and insulting. But, good God, I am much too*
> *mild in insulting such devils"*-- Of The Unknowable Name and The
> Generations of Christ

John Calvin **(1509-1564)**

Their [the Jews] rotten and unbending stiffneckedness deserves that they be
oppressed unendingly and without measure or end and that they die in their
misery without the pity of anyone."-- Ad Quaelstiones et Objecta Juaei
Cuiusdam Responsio

The Middle Ages

By the Middle Ages, two erroneous and deadly concepts had become established Church doctrine:

1. The Jews should be considered "Christ killers" and should be mistreated accordingly.

2. The Church has replaced Israel, and God has no future purpose for the Jews.

These concepts were reinforced throughout the Middle Ages through the Crusades, the Inquisition and passion plays. Jews were accused of poisoning water wells, causing the black plague epidemic, leading to the merciless slaughter of untold millions of Jewish innocents. The evidence pointed to was the fact that while Gentiles were subject to contracting the disease, Jews were seemingly unaffected. The answer must be that Jews were the cause, never mind the fact that they were insulated from the disease simply because they kept the laws of cleanliness prescribed by the Torah.

The justification for Jewish persecutions through the centuries has been a passage from the Matthew gospel. After Pilate denied responsibility for sentencing Jesus to death, the Jewish people are quoted as saying *" His blood be on us, and on our children"* (Matthew 27:25). A similar theme may be found at 1 Thessalonians 2:15. In Christian eyes this meant that the Jews as a race were collectively responsible for the death of Jesus. In time, the principle of collective guilt would open the way to the assignment of other imaginary forms of guilt. The fact that Jesus had been a Jew, as his parents and his followers had been, was overlooked. In Christian art the Jews were depicted as ugly and deformed, while Jesus was a handsome blue-eyed blond-haired European.

In 1095 Pope Urban II called for a crusade to deliver the Holy Land from Islamic rule. The primary goal of the crusade was to liberate Jerusalem from the Muslims, however Jews were a second target in the process. Years of institutional hatred and fear resulting from claims that Jews committed deicide culminated in one of the worst horrific periods of genocidal mania in history.

The abbot of Cluny fanned the flames of anti-Semitic hatred when he asked the question, *"why should Christians travel to the ends of the world to fight the*

Saracens, when we permit among us other infidels a thousand times more guilty toward Christ than the Mohammedans?" The floodgates burst wide open, giving rise to violent mobs who set about cleansing the land of Jews, murdering thousands of men, women and children to the cry of *"Conversion or death!"* This genocidal mania persisted through eight additional crusades until the the last one in the year 1272.

Passion plays became a popular form of entertainment during the Middle Ages, adding fuel to a culture of Jew hatred. Jews were depicted as demons who knew full well that Christ was the son of God. In each play, as Christ carried the cross, he was tortured by bloodthirsty, cursing devils with hooked noses, horns and tails. The Jews were made to seem as the very epitome of evil and were treated accordingly.

It became commonplace among Christian groups to think of Jews as agents of Satan. One widely accepted anti-Jewish fable was the idea of blood libel, that Jews murdered Christians each year around the time of Passover to get blood used in performing satanic rites. Another lie commonly circulated was that Jews stole the wafers used in communion in order to stab them with knives, killing Christ again and again.

During that span of time, more than sixty Jewish communities were burned to the ground, their occupants murdered and many times tortured and burned to death in bonfires - all in the name of the Prince of Peace - by Christians.

In 1478, Pope Sixtus IV granted the monarchs of Spain, Ferdinand and Isabella, the right to establish a special inquisition in Spain to deal with baptized Jews who were suspected of remaining faithful to Judaism. Thousands were burned at the stake by order of the Spanish Inquisition. In 1492, King Ferdinand ordered that all Jews were to be expelled from Spain as they posed a danger to Christianity.

The Impact of the Reformation on Anti-Semitism

Unfortunately, the Reformation produced no real changes in attitude towards Jews. In fact, Jew hatred was reinforced by the writings of Martin Luther, the very man who launched the Reformation. Luther initially believed the Jews' rejection of Christ was due to their recognition of the corruption of the Roman Catholic Church. However, when they continued to reject the Gospel, Luther unleashed a torrent of verbal and literary attacks on them. In 1543 he wrote the afore-mentioned pamphlet entitled <u>Concerning The Jews and Their Lies.</u> The document was an anti-Semitic diatribe worthy of Hitler himself. In it, he referred to the Jews as:

- *"A miserable and accursed people"*
- *"Stupid fools"*
- *"Miserable, blind and senseless"*
- *"Thieves and robbers"*
- *"The great vermin of humanity"*
- *"Lazy rogues"*
- *"Blind and venomous"*

Having joined with his predecessors in dehumanizing and demonizing the Jews, Luther then proceeds to make some startling suggestions on how to deal with them:

- Their synagogues and schools should be burned.
- Their houses should be destroyed.
- Their Talmudic writings should be confiscated.
- Their Rabbis should be forbidden to teach.
- Their money should be taken from them.
- They should be compelled into forced labor.

Sounds much like the rhetoric spewed from the mouths of Islamic scholars, whom history shows were complicit and instrumental in Adolf Hitler's "final solution", the destruction of the Jewish people. Nazi propaganda included quotes from Luther as they rose to power and launched the Holocaust. In his book <u>Mein Kampf</u>, published in 1925, Hitler referred to Martin Luther as *"a great warrior, a true statesmen, and a great reformer."* Keep in mind that <u>Hitler was a professed Christian.</u>

At a Christian gathering in Berlin in 1924, Hitler received a standing ovation when he made the following declaration: "*I believe that today I am acting in accordance with the will of Almighty God as I announce the most important work that Christians could undertake - and that is to be against the Jews and get rid of them once and for all.*" He then talked about the influence Luther had on his life: "*Martin Luther has been the greatest encouragement of my life. Luther was a great man.*

He was a giant. With one blow he heralded the coming of the new dawn and the new age. He saw clearly that the Jews need to be destroyed, and we're only beginning to see that we need to carry this work on."

At the Nuremberg trials after World War II, Julius Streicher, speaking in defense of his actions during the war, said *"I have never said anything that Martin Luther did not say."*

The terrible truth that many Christians are unaware of and perhaps are unwilling to confront is that the Holocaust was the result of 1,800 years of virulent Christian anti-Semitism.

The New Anti-Semitism

The horror of the Holocaust had the effect of dampening the most radical anti-Semitic speech among Christian leaders. But in reality, anti-Semitism continues today in a new sophisticated form called anti-Zionism. Whereas anti-Semitism attempted to drive the Jews from the lands where they lived, anti-Zionism refuses to accept their right to live in their own land.

A good example of the new anti-Semitism can be found in an open letter addressed to Evangelicals by Dr. James Kennedy of the Knox Theological Seminary. In this document, dated in 2002, he expresses his beliefs concerning the land of Israel. It has since been endorsed by hundreds of theologians and pastors, including contemporary theological giants like R. C. Sproul.

The document begins by denouncing those who teach that the Bible's promises concerning the land of Israel are being fulfilled today *"in a special region or* 'Holy Land,' *perpetually set apart by God for one ethnic group alone."* It then proceeds to proclaim that the promises made to Abraham *"do not apply to any particular ethnic group, but to the church of Jesus Christ, **the true Israel**"*. As with most errors in doctrinal debate, that statement is only partially true. The Abrahamic Covenant is indeed given to all who believe in the Messiah of Israel, regardless of ethnic bloodline. The error comes in the comment *"the true Israel, the Church"*, a clear reference to replacement theology, replacing Israel and granting the Covenant promises to the New Testament Church.

He continues by specifically rejecting the Jew's claim to any land in the Middle East: *"The entitlement of any one ethnic or religious group to territory in the Middle East called the 'Holy Land' cannot be supported by Scripture."* How does one escape the plethora of scriptures pointing to an end time return of the Jews to the Promised Land? Simply assert that *"the land promises specific to Israel in the Old Testament were fulfilled under Joshua.".* Then grant those promises to the Church and voila! A healthy dose of Jew-be-gone is applied to any reference to physical fulfillment of prophecy, scrubbed and white-washed and replaced with the new and improved Covenant.

Adding salt to the wounds, the document concludes with the following observation:

"The present secular state of Israel is not an authentic or prophetic realization of the Messianic kingdom of Jesus Christ. Furthermore, a day should not be anticipated in which Christ's kingdom will manifest Jewish distinctives, whether by its location in 'the land' by its constituency, or by its ceremonial institutions and practices." Never mind the numerous passages wherein the promises of God to Israel are declared to be without repentance, i.e. Jer 31:36 *"If those ordinances depart from before me, saith the LORD, then the seed of Israel also shall cease from being a nation before me forever."* Never mind that prophecies concerning the Millennial Kingdom are rife with references to a restoration of the Feasts of the Lord, the keeping of Sabbath and many other "Jewish" activities.

In a nutshell, there it is, an overview of the un-Christ-like sordid history of Christian anti-Semitism, rooted in Replacement Theology which persists to this day under the guise of anti-Zionism. Is it any wonder that the whole world seems to be aligning itself, with the United Nations leading the charge, against the right of Jews to exist as a nation?

The Jewish Attitude

Is it any wonder why Jews look with suspicion when we try to share the Gospel with them? Because Jews have been persecuted and killed throughout history in the name of Jesus, the Jewish people look upon Christianity as their mortal enemy.

Any Jew who converts to Christianity is considered a traitor, for he is viewed as one who has joined the enemy. That's the reason that Orthodox

Jews react so strongly to a child who becomes a Christian. They will sometimes declare the child to be dead and will even conduct a funeral service.

This is the reason that the Messianic Jewish Movement today is such a miracle.

Appeal to Scripture

What does the Word of God have to say about all this? To begin with, it strongly repudiates anti-Semitism. Psalm 129:5-8 says that *"all who hate Zion"* will be *"put to shame..."* It further states that no believer should ever give a blessing to such a person.

With regard to the allegation that the Jews are "Christ killers," the Word clearly identifies who murdered Jesus and makes it plain that they were not exclusively the Jews. In Acts 4:27 we are told that Jesus was killed through a conspiracy that involved "both Herod and Pontius Pilate, along with the Gentiles and the peoples of Israel." In reality, all of us have the blood of Jesus on our hands, for all of us have sinned[68] and Jesus died for all sinners (1 Corinthians 15:3).

The inconvenient truth is that I crucified Christ. I and you and every other human being on the planet were the cause of his death. The Jews didn't kill him. The Romans didn't kill him. He could have called forth ten thousand times ten thousand mighty angels to rescue him, but he didn't. It was love alone that held him suspended between Heaven and Earth to pay for your sins and mine.

An amazing macro revelation of God's foreknowledge and wisdom in working out His plan of salvation through history is seen in the fact that all three of the people groups who came out of Shem, Ham and Japheth were represented at the crucifixion. They are seen at his birth as well as countless other events throughout history. Is it possible what is viewed by many as the curse of Ham might actually be considered a blessing? Ham was cursed to be a *"servant of servants"* and as people groups spread around the world from the plains of Shinar after the Tower of Babel incident, it can be shown

---

[68] Romans 3:23 "For all have sinned, and come short of the glory of God;"

that the Hamitic peoples indeed served as servants of mankind. It was Hamitic peoples who led the way in conquering new territories, making new discoveries like smelting and tool making, all in preparation for the Shemites and Japhethites who would follow in due course.

Another clue of this possibility is understanding a literary device used in the Hebrew language to expand a comparative idea with a superlative, using phrases like Lord of Lords, King of Kings and so on. Jesus was indeed the Servant of all servants. To give further evidence, by amazing coincidence, it was one Simeon, a Hamitic descendant, who was pressed into helping Jesus carry His cross on the way to Calvary.

Regarding the idea that God has already fulfilled the land promises to the Jews during the time of Joshua, it is interesting to note that long after Joshua, David wrote in the psalms that the land promise is everlasting in nature and is yet to be fulfilled (Psalm 105:8-11). The fact of the matter is that the Jews have never occupied all the land that was promised to them in the Abrahamic Covenant (Genesis 15:18-21) so for Israel to fulfill that promise, ALL of the land must be occupied. That is yet future.

Anti-Semitism is widespread, virulent and completely irrational. Why does it persist? Because it is a supernatural phenomenon.

Satan hates the Jews. He hates them because through the Jews came the promised Seed of the Woman who would crush the seed of the Serpent. He hates them because the Scriptures came through and has been preserved by them. He hates them because God promised to save a great remnant of them. He hates them because God promised to build His kingdom around them after destroying the Devil's own kingdom. He hates them because God loves them. It really is as simple as that.

His hatred drives him to plant seeds of mistrust and hatred in people's hearts toward the Jews. He is determined to destroy every Jew on planet earth so that God cannot keep His promise to save a great remnant. He tried to annihilate them beginning with Cain and Abel; he tried with Moses, with Amalek, with Haman in Esther, with the crucifixion, in the Holocaust. Countless time he's tried and countless times he failed. He is trying to destroy them today and will make his ultimate attempt during the last half of the Great Tribulation. He will fail again.

Concerning the claim that the Jews have been rejected by God, there are a couple of biblical principles that need to be kept in mind.

First, the Bible affirms that Israel was called as God's Chosen People to be witnesses to the world of God's desire to commune on a personal level with mankind.[69] And the Bible makes it clear that this calling is **irrevocable**.[70]

Second, in direct contradiction of Replacement Theology, the Bible teaches that the Jews have never been rejected by God because of their unbelief. In Romans 3 Paul asserts point blank that their rejection of Jesus has not nullified God's faithfulness to the promises He made to them.[71] Paul makes the point again when he asks, *"I say then, Hath God cast away his people?"*[72] He answers his own question emphatically with *"God forbid!"* He then states *"God hath not cast away his people which he foreknew."*[73] It is true that the Jewish people are currently under discipline because of their rejection of their Messiah. Over and over in their Scriptures the prophets said they would be disciplined if they were unfaithful, but always the promise was made that they would be preserved. An example of this type of prophetic statement

---

[69] Isa 43:10 Ye are my witnesses, saith the LORD, and my servant whom I have chosen: that ye may know and believe me, and understand that I am he: before me there was no God formed, neither shall there be after me.
Isa 43:11 I, even I, am the LORD; and beside me there is no saviour.
Isa 43:12 I have declared, and have saved, and I have shewed, when there was no strange god among you: therefore ye are my witnesses, saith the LORD, that I am God.
[70] Rom 11:26 And so all Israel shall be saved: as it is written, There shall come out of Sion the Deliverer, and shall turn away ungodliness from Jacob:
Rom 11:27 For this is my covenant unto them, when I shall take away their sins.
Rom 11:28 As concerning the gospel, they are enemies for your sakes: but as touching the election, they are beloved for the fathers' sakes.
Rom 11:29 For the gifts and calling of God are without repentance.
[71] Romans 3:1-4 "What advantage then hath the Jew? or what profit *is there* of circumcision? Much every way: chiefly, because that unto them were committed the oracles of God. For what if some did not believe? shall their unbelief make the faith of God without effect? God forbid: yea, let God be true, but every man a liar; as it is written, That thou mightest be justified in thy sayings, and mightest overcome when thou art judged.
[72] Romans 11:1
[73] Romans 11:2

can be found in Jeremiah.[74]

God has preserved them in His grace because He loves them. In Zechariah 2:8 God proclaims that the Jewish people are *"the apple of His eye,"* and He warns against anyone trying to harm them.

The promise is made repeatedly throughout the Hebrew Scriptures and confirmed by Paul in the New Testament that a great remnant of Jews would be saved in the last days. The salvation of this remnant is described in detail in Zechariah 12:10 where it says that at the end of the Tribulation the remaining Jews will come to the end of themselves and will turn their hearts to God in repentance and accept Jesus as their Messiah.

A believing remnant[75] will go into the Millennium in the flesh and will comprise the nation of Israel through whom God will fulfill all the promises He declared in the Old Testament. During the Millennium, Israel will fulfill her destiny as the one nation through whom God will bless all the other nations.[76]

Conclusion

God is in control, not Satan. God has the wisdom and power to orchestrate

---

[74] Jer 30:11 For I am with thee, saith the LORD, to save thee: though I make a full end of all nations whither I have scattered thee, yet will I not make a full end of thee: but I will correct thee in measure, and will not leave thee altogether unpunished.

[75] Isa 10:20 And it shall come to pass in that day, that the remnant of Israel, and such as are escaped of the house of Jacob, shall no more again stay upon him that smote them; but shall stay upon the LORD, the Holy One of Israel, in truth.
Isa 10:21 The remnant shall return, even the remnant of Jacob, unto the mighty God.
Isa 10:22 For though thy people Israel be as the sand of the sea, yet a remnant of them shall return: the consumption decreed shall overflow with righteousness.

[76] Zec 8:22 Yea, many people and strong nations shall come to seek the LORD of hosts in Jerusalem, and to pray before the LORD.
Zec 8:23 Thus saith the LORD of hosts; In those days it shall come to pass, that ten men shall take hold out of all languages of the nations, even shall take hold of the skirt of him that is a Jew, saying, We will go with you: for we have heard that God is with you.

all the evil of Satan and Mankind to the triumph of His perfect will in history.

The Jews will be preserved. A great remnant will be saved. All the promises to the Jews will be fulfilled.

And when will this occur? At the end of the Tribulation when Jesus returns to triumph over Satan. On that glorious day, the Jewish remnant will cry out "Baruch Haba B'ha'shem Adonai!" meaning "Blessed is He who comes in the name of the Lord!" (Matthew 23:39).

In summary, the Word of God makes it clear that Israel definitely has a role and a future in the end times.

8
DISPENSATIONAL THEOLOGY

Once the inseparable Word of God is dismantled and artificially divided into two competing streams of theology, i.e., *law* versus *grace*, the whole counsel of God is then subject to all manner of errant interpretation.

In the early years of ministry, I bit into the dispensational interpretation of Scripture hook, line and sinker. Why? Because truthfully it sounded so reasonable and let's face it, it made for darn good sermon material. But the bottom line is, in a word, one chooses to believe it, as is true in all matters of faith. What I was taught by my early mentor, he learned from his mentor who learned from his all the way back to a relatively recent specific point in history. A seriously flawed and un-Biblical teaching that did **not** originate with the writers of the New Testament took Christianity by storm in the midst of one of the greatest revivals in American history. What those inspired witnesses of the first century passed on to subsequent generations was the teaching that came directly from Jesus Himself. That simple teaching was intended to be passed on by His disciples and the disciples of their disciples through every succeeding generation. However, Satan does as Satan is. With one stroke of his deceptive pen he convinced the early Church to embark on a path of private interpretation of Scripture that ultimately led to the great divide between Israel and the Church. The simple but deceptive phrase "*hath God said*" had the same devastating effect it has always had on God's people: did God really mean what is simply written in His Word, or must we look to a religious authority to rightly understand truth? The very idea of a clergy/laity religious hierarchy is built upon this fraud; that the common person is unable and therefore should not attempt to interpret Scripture without appealing to a properly trained and appointed spiritual head to understand the mysteries of God's Word.

That is not to say there is no place for spiritual leadership. The point is, you and I by our very nature are easily led and thus risk, like all sheep, being led astray by various winds of doctrine and errant philosophies. We must take care to prove everything we hear and say by the Word of God. Test the church fathers, test your pastor, test the substance of this book. Test your own thoughts and beliefs. Test everything! In the end, let God be God and truth be our singular pursuit, regardless of whether it fits our current understanding and belief or not.

What It Is

Dispensationalism sees God as unfolding His Plan of Salvation for mankind through a series of progressive and cumulative revelations, each successive period building upon the previous dispensation. In each dispensation, mankind is given stewardship as a test to be faithful to the particular revelation given at the time. Mankind fails to live up to the requirements of each dispensation, which finally leads to judgment at which time mankind is transitioned into a new dispensation with its specific requirements for faithfulness, failure and eventual judgment.

In essence dispensational theology teaches that God divided the entire history of mankind into seven distinct dispensations, or ages, each with its own specific responsibility for obedience, each with its own failures of mankind to keep those requirements, and each with a specific judgment for that failure.

These so-called dispensations were designated proper names to distinguish and highlight their differences.

1. Innocence – from creation to the Fall.
2. Conscience -- from the Fall to the Flood.
3. Human government -- from the Flood to Abram
4. Promise – from Abraham to the giving of the Law at Mt. Sinai.
5. Law – From Sinai to the Cross of Christ.
6. Grace -- from the death of Christ to the judgments in Revelation.
7. Kingdom or Millennial Age -- the restoration of the Davidic kingdom during which Christ will reign one thousand years. [#7 is the only "dispensation" designation the author agrees with]

Dispensational theology, with its artificial demarcations, embraces a distinction between Israel and the Church. Accordingly, the promises made to Israel in the Old Testament were not intended as prophetic of how God would accomplish in the Messiah the formation of one new man, the Body of Christ made up of Jew and Gentile. Instead, the promises to Israel will be literally fulfilled by physical Israel itself in the millennial age. The promise of the land is interpreted to mean that God will one day fulfill for Israel an earthly inheritance whereas the Church's inheritance is a heavenly one.

Although both Jews and Gentiles are saved by Christ through faith, believing Israel will be the recipient of earthly promises, with the restoration of national Israel in the specific land promised to their forefathers, while the promise to believing Gentiles is an inheritance of heavenly rewards. It is thus accurate to say that dispensationalism teaches there are two peoples of God with two distinct promises and two separate fulfillments. How's that for an elaborate reconstruction of a wall of division that Paul took such great pains to tear down?[77]

In contrast, non-dispensationalists typically see the land promise as intended by God to prophesy, in shadow and type, the greater reality that He would one day make the entire church, Jew and Gentile, heirs of the whole renewed world. Romans 4:13 says *"For the promise, that he should be the heir of the world, was not to Abraham, or to his seed, through the law, but through the righteousness of faith."* Replacement theologians will interpret this passage as proof of a distinction between law and faith, when the focus should be on the antecedent subject, that Abraham and his seed would inherit the world!

Once again the Church is brought to utter confusion in accepting interpretations of Scripture with a pre-determined doctrinal position conceived in the muddled hermeneutics of early theologians with a decidedly anti-Semitic bias.

Paul the apostle gave instruction to *rightly divide*[78] the word of truth. That means **you** are responsible to rightly interpret God's Word; **you alone** are responsible to search the Scriptures daily to prove whether these things are so; **you alone** are accountable to allow God's Word to speak for itself

---

[77] Eph 2:14 For he is our peace, who hath made both one, and hath broken down the middle wall of partition between us;

[78] 2Ti 2:15 Study to shew thyself approved unto God, a workman that needeth not to be ashamed, rightly dividing the word of truth.

without forcing contradictory interpretations into the text. If you have to spiritualize plain text in order for it to fit a predetermined outcome; if your interpretation causes contradictions in the immutable Word of God, you're doing it wrong! If you'll go back and prayerfully study the offending text with an open mind and teachable spirit, you will find that any perceived contradictions simply disappear!

In this passage, the word translated *rightly divide* in both Greek and Hebrew, is a single word that means to make a straight cut or to stand upright. The Hebrew is even more telling. The word is yashar, which shares same root the name Yeshua comes from. The meaning in Paul's mind is that to rightly divide the Word of Truth is to properly interpret the Word according to how Jesus, who is the *"word made flesh"*[79] interpreted it.

Lest one think Paul was using words that were re-defined to fit a new theological paradigm, consider carefully what he said in his letter to Timothy about the foundation of all theology, doctrine and instructions in righteousness.[80] Remember too that the only **all scripture** that existed at the time of writing was the Tanach, or the Old Testament.

Don't take your pastor's word for it. He learned it from his seminary teacher, who learned it from his seminary teacher who learned it from his teacher before him. The simplicity that was passed down from **the** teacher eventually morphed into dispensational theology and a myriad of other basic theological constructs, all built upon the insidious and precarious foundation of replacement theology. What did Jesus say about that? A house built on shifting sand cannot stand. The Church found herself stripped and naked, on shifting sand of theological interpretations carefully crafted by the enemy to strip the Body of its only offensive and defensive weapon, the unchanging Word of God. Somewhere early along the line there was a disturbance in the ether and the signal has been garbled ever since.

Friend, I beg you. Come back to your Biblical roots as **you** study to show **yourself** approved unto God. No one else will be standing with you at the Judgment Seat of Christ to account for how you interpreted, or *mis*interpreted as it were, God's Word to you. Let no man rob you of your reward.

---

[79] Joh 1:14 And the Word was made flesh, and dwelt among us ...
[80] 2Ti 3:16 All scripture is given by inspiration of God, and is profitable for doctrine, for reproof, for correction, for instruction in righteousness:

Dispensations: Word of God or Word of Man?

If the Bible does not teach dispensational doctrine, where does it come from? Quite bluntly, much of the Church's teaching on the subject comes from C.I. Scofield's commentary on the Bible, not the Bible itself. He gives no scriptural authority for there is none to be found. These divisions are arbitrary and they all overlap. God made a promise in Eden of a Coming One. Adam had a conscience and he hid out of shame for his disobedience. God met him at his point of need and covered his sins by grace. Did conscience cease to function at the end of that particular dispensational precept? Did human government cease to exist at the end of its particular age? Did the Age of Promise evolve into an Age of Law, which would then give way to an Age of Grace, and then re-emerge as a Kingdom Age wherein is found the fulfillment of all the dispensational requirements and their respective failures, judgments and replacements? That's silly on the face of it. No one can be saved apart from God's grace in any age. Our Father's demands for obedience are the same in every age; that is, to do justly, to love kindness and to walk humbly before our God. (Micah 6:8). These were the weightier matters of the law Jesus referred to in confronting the hypocrisy of the Pharisees.

Two Destructive Dispensations

The two artificially designated dispensations that had the most insidious and devastating effect on God's people and the transmission of the simple teaching that Jesus passed down to His disciples are those called *"The Dispensation of Law"* and *"The Dispensation of Grace"*.

With one stroke, the liar of all liars split the cohesive, interconnected revelation of the mind of God which we call the Bible, into a fragmented patchwork of man's baseless interpretations that Paul in no way intended to be divided. (See above definition of *divide*)

This false division in the Word of God has caused immeasurable harm to the Body of Christ. Interpretations of Paul's writing are twisted to mean things that are totally contrary to not only other passages of Scripture, but Paul's own writings end up contradicting each other!

We will discuss these two concepts more in depth in a later chapter.

Origin of Dispensational Theology

There were two key players in the formulation and rapid advancement of dispensational teaching. A man by the name of John Nelson Darby was the person responsible for formulating a distinct dispensational method for interpreting Scripture. The most zealous advocate of Darby's "new" understanding of Biblical interpretation was none other than Charles Ingersoll Scofield of Scofield Study Bible fame referenced above.

The history of these two is a textbook study in the persuasive power of the Deceiver to distort and manipulate the pure and holy Word of God to fit a predetermined belief.

Darby was born November 18, 1800 in London, England. With an extremely low opinion of the Protestant Reformers and an equally arrogant high regard for his own intelligence, he decided he could better interpret Scripture than those who came before. His self-acclaimed correct method for interpreting the prophetic literature of the Old Testament eventually evolved into what is known today as *Dispensational Theology*.

Many in the nineteenth century Protestant Church who knew him made comments about him with words such as *"weird little man"* and *"personally revolting"*, yet at the same time found his Biblical interpretation irresistible. As one writer describes him, the hold he had on people seemed almost cultic in its effect. *"In spite of the strong revulsion which I felt against some of the peculiarities of this remarkable man, I for the first time in my life found myself under the dominion of a superior. When I remember, how even those bowed down before him, who had been to him in the place of parents-accomplished and experienced minds-I cease to wonder in the retrospect, that he riveted me in such bondage."* - Francis W. Newman, Phases of Faith p. 54) Perhaps more discerning minds might have taken that personality trait as a clue to the probable author of Darby's novel approach.

Like the Protestant Reformers before him, Darby insisted some critical truth had been lost in the Church and his purpose in life was to find and restore that truth. However, unlike the other Reformers, who based their theology on the writings of earlier generations of Christians, Darby was so convinced of the superiority of his own intelligence, he discarded altogether the interpretations of those who came before and devised his own personal system of hermeneutics. Where Calvin and others sought to restore things they believed had been lost based on the writings of Augustine and earlier church fathers, Darby's interpretations introduced to the Church a whole new truth extracted from the depths of his own mind.

His disdain for the early Church theologians was clearly stated this way: *"None are more untrustworthy on every fundamental subject than the mass of primitive Fathers."*[81] As we'll see shortly, his explanations were so powerfully convincing, they were and are accepted as Church dogma in many of today's denominations.

Bible teachers who espouse this doctrine imply that primitive Christianity had a rudimentary grasp of dispensationalism, but the full knowledge only evolved over a period of eighteen hundred years. In other words, the Church had to wait for eighteen centuries before someone of Darby's supreme spiritual insight was raised up to fully teach the truth that was lost shortly after the first century.

According to the traditional Protestant position, the Early Church had the Truth and lost it sometime after the Apostolic Age. Therefore, they saw the task of the Protestant theologian as an attempt to determine what Truth had been lost and to restore it. The Protestant Reformers did right by coming out of the Papal bondage that had held the Children of God captive for centuries. However, it is the premise of this book that they only came part way out. It is time to finish the Restoration and come all the way out of Babylonian tradition. The Church did indeed veer from the path of Truth, but it is this writer's opinion that the Truth that was lost was the simple teaching that Jesus gave to His Apostles, the Truth that was rooted and grounded in the only Scripture in existence at the time, the Old Testament.

Darby himself said about the Early Church Fathers which included the likes of Hippolytus, a disciple of the apostle John: *"For my own part, if I were bound to receive all that has been said by the Millenarians, I would reject the whole system: but their views and statements weigh with me not one feather. But this does not hinder me from inquiring* **by the teaching of the same Spirit ... what God has with**

---

81 The Collected Writings of J. N. Darby [Sunbury, Pa.: Believers Bookshelf, 1971], Vol. 14, Ecc. No. 3, p. 68)

infinite graciousness revealed to me concerning His dealing with the Church. I confess I think the modern writers on prophecy justly chargeable with following their own thoughts hastily, and far too removed from the control of the Scripture ... They take some text or prophecy as a starting point, pursue these suggestions of their minds in connection with their general views previously adopted, but leave the results almost entirely untried by the direct testimony of the Word, affording us theories ... diverging into the absurdities.... There is not a single writer whose writings I have seen (unless it be the author of one short inquiry) who is not chargeable with this fault.[82] [Emphasis added]

Talk about the pot calling the kettle black!

Darby's condescension toward earlier generations of Church leaders and modern writers as well is clear in the pronouncement of his "Spirit taught" revelation emphasized in the above quote. Seeking private interpretation[83] of Scripture is a dangerous undertaking. The Deceiver is more than happy to oblige the seeker with enough truth mixed with lies to make the interpretation enticing. In Darby's case, nearly the whole Church was infected with his wrong-headed private theology. If an interpretation is not in full agreement with the rest of Scripture, it must be studied again and again until it is brought into alignment with the whole counsel of God. Scripture does not contradict itself.

How Darby the Man Became Darby the Prophet

Like many Protestants of that era, Darby was a member of the Anglican Church. He graduated from Trinity College in Dublin, Ireland in 1819, practicing law for a number of years before being "called" to the ministry. He was ordained as a deacon in 1825 and the following year was ordained an Anglican priest.

Apparently dissatisfied with the orthodoxy of the Church of England, he left the Anglican Church, meeting with a group calling themselves the Brethren, later becoming known as the Plymouth Brethren. Like Darby, the

SB, NE

---

[82] - (J. N. Darby, "Reflections Upon the Prophetic Inquiry, and the Views Advanced in It," pp. 6–7, quoted by Bass, p. 128).

[83] 2Pe 1:20-21 Knowing this first, that no prophecy of the scripture is of any private interpretation. For the prophecy came not in old time by the will of man: but holy men of God spake as they were moved by the Holy Ghost.

group was made up of former members of the Church of England who had a few years earlier left the Church to start their own movement.

Darby's affiliation with the Plymouth Brethren provided fertile ground for developing his own views concerning eschatology regarding the Church. His brand new personal method of interpretation of the prophecies served to widen the chasm between Israel and the Church created by the early Replacement Theologians. The essence of Dispensational Theology was not concerned with Biblical truths about sin, salvation, the nature of God, church government or even the cohesive nature of the Word of God itself. Its central concern was and is eschatology, a method of interpreting prophetic scripture.

His teaching found limited exposure until 1947 when Lewis Sperry Chafer published Darby's prophetic system as a systematic theology on the order of Calvinism, Methodism etc. Dispensational views concerning the Antichrist and the second coming of Jesus Christ then quickly spread to every corner of Christianity and was assimilated into many other theological systems. Over a short period of time, this new eschatological system uprooted and replaced much of traditional Christian teaching of prophetic interpretation.

Israel Is the Jews

Or is it?

The heart of the dispensationalists' interest in interpreting the Scriptures is their identification of the Jews as the literal Israel spoken of by the Prophets. Covenant Theology and Dispensational Theology differ in their understanding of the relationship between Israel and the Church. Covenant theologians adhere to the traditional Christian view that the Church is spiritual Israel, whereas dispensationalists uphold Darby's claim that the Jews are literal Israel and there is no spiritual Israel. However, in our view, neither side has a completely accurate understanding of the truth of the scriptural message. The truth is, Jesus Christ is literal Israel,[84] the root and branch out of dry ground into which all the redeemed are grafted. The Church, both Jew and Gentile, is metaphorically His spiritual body.

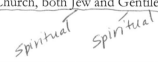

spiritual   spiritual

---

[84] Isa 49:3 And said unto me, Thou art my servant, O Israel, in whom I will be glorified.

108

As simple and straight forward as this premise might be, Darby's prophetic system convinced most of the Evangelical Church that the Jews are literal Israel and the Church should not be identified with Israel in any way. In perfect agreement with Origen, who introduced his folly around A.D. 200, Satan has enticed the Church into fuzzy thinking concerning the identity of literal Israel. Even John Calvin was sucked into that vortex by what Augustine had written. Consequently, he exhibited a decided ambivalence concerning the Jews and what, if any, role they continued to play in God's plan.

It is the classic logical premise: all rabbits are quadrupeds but not all quadrupeds are rabbits. All Jews are Israelites but not all Israelites are Jews. All Israel is comprised of Judah, Ephraim (northern ten tribes) as well as believing Gentiles.

The Church suffers from separation anxiety. The long history of identifying the Jews as Israel, a mistake the vast majority of Christians make today, further cements the disconnect between the Church and Israel. That may have been the catalyst that prompted Darby to publish his first work that same year. In it, he contended that every mention of Israel in the Prophets refers to the Jews.

A few years after Darby joined the Plymouth Brethren, Alexander Campbell and Barton Stone withdrew from the Baptists to form the Disciples of Christ (1830–32According to the Scriptures, the Messiah is literal Israel, Heir to all The Promises of God. The Church is spiritual Israel only in the sense that it is metaphorically the spiritual Body of Jesus Christ. Therefore, contrary to what most folks believe, Jesus Christ is both literal Israel and spiritual Israel.

The Imminent Return of Christ

By the time Darby published The Hopes of the Church of God in 1840, his beliefs concerning the future of Israel and the Church were becoming fundamental doctrine among the Plymouth Brethren, spreading rapidly through local congregations in America and abroad.

But all was not smooth sailing for Darby's push to find acceptance of his "new" prophetic system. In 1845, B.W. Newton, another prominent leader among the Brethren, came under attack by Darby because he dared to disagree with one of his new doctrines. This doctrine found great appeal in much of the Body of Christ and since then spread like wildfire into virtually every pocket of Christianity, becoming almost a salvation issue in many denominations. Newton adamantly rejected Darby's teaching on the pre-tribulation Rapture of the saints. The idea that the Rapture could occur at any moment was not a widespread belief in Christianity prior to this dispute with Newton. And for good reason. The only others teaching the doctrine was a group known as the Irvingites, named for their leader, Edward Irving. It's no wonder most Christians reject the notion that their belief in a pre-trib rapture came from Darby, and Darbyites deny getting the doctrine from Irving considering his wacky views on prophecy. Irrespective of all denials though, the teachings are identical. There can be little doubt Darby was exposed to the teachings of Irving during prophetic conferences he attended in London in the 1830s.

The only other mention of a pre-tribulation rapture of the Church before being taught by Edward Irving and his followers is a brief mention by Joseph Meade in 1677 in response to a question he had received. Even he didn't teach it as a doctrine, only as speculation in his answer to the query.

RAPTURE

Irving taught in 1825 that the members of his Catholic Apostolic Church would soon restrain the power of the anti-Christ for 3 ½ years, after which they would be martyred and ascend en masse to heaven. He also stated his followers would then return with Christ in the clouds of glory at the end of the 3 ½ year reign of the anti-Christ. Not many years later, one William Miller would take up the mantle of the imminent return doctrine, which we'll discuss later in the chapter.

Nevertheless, the pre-tribulation rapture of the saints is clearly what Irving preached, albeit today we would call it a mid-tribulation rapture, or in the middle of the seventieth week of Daniel but before the Great Tribulation spoken of by Jesus.[85] Despite denials to the contrary, Darby apparently modified a doctrine borrowed from Irving to include in his dispensational teaching.

The vast majority of modern Christians have been so thoroughly

---

[85] Mat 24:21 For then shall be great tribulation, such as was not since the beginning of the world to this time, no, nor ever shall be.

indoctrinated into the "at any moment" return of Christ doctrine that most will never stop to consider it might not be Biblical. Modern Christians, if they actually take time to trace the roots of the "any moment" doctrine, will dismiss the idea that Miller, Irving et al were wrong in their doctrine but insist they were simply wrong in their timing. A common refrain in local churches of virtually every denominational stripe is "Be ready! Jesus could come tomorrow!" But is that true? Could He really return just any old time?

Consider this: Jesus was crucified on the Biblical feast of Passover. He was laid in the tomb at the beginning of the Biblical feast of Unleavened Bread. He then rose from the grave on the Biblical day of First Fruits. Fifty days later, He ascended into Heaven and sent the Holy Spirit on the Biblical feast of Shavuot, what we today call Pentecost. All four Biblically mandated celebrations were fulfilled perfectly by Jesus at His first advent on the very day and hour of the Biblical feasts according to Scripture. Three of the seven were un-fulfilled at that time, the feast of Trumpets, Day of Atonement and the feast of Tabernacles. Is it really a stretch to believe He will fulfill the last three at His second coming? I asked a prominent pastor in the town where I lived at the time years ago if he thought the fact that Jesus fulfilled all four of the first feasts was just coincidence. His response? Yes, it was purely coincidental and had no bearing on the second coming. What? Are you kidding me? My reply to that is simple: coincidence is not a kosher word! God does nothing by happenstance, and in my opinion, the Devil has masterfully blinded most in the Church to the truth of His glorious return and the reality in the prophetic types presented in His Biblical Feasts.

Sadly, the vast majority of Christians, many of them dear friends of mine, buy into the "any moment" belief, never mind that passages like 1st Corinthians 15[86] and 1st Thessalonians 4[87] clearly connect the second coming of Jesus to the Feast of Trumpets.

---

[86] 1Co 15:52 In a moment, in the twinkling of an eye, at the last trump: for the trumpet shall sound, and the dead shall be raised incorruptible, and we shall be changed.

[87] 1Th 4:16 For the Lord himself shall descend from heaven with a shout, with the voice of the archangel, and with the trump of God: and the dead in Christ shall rise first:

Back to Darby: when Newton disputed his imminent return view of the rapture, the two exchanged a series of nasty arguments and after parting company, Darby soon organized an offshoot of the Brethren. This new exclusive sect sought to maintain doctrinal purity, refusing to fellowship with anyone who disagreed with Darby's brand of prophetic interpretation, especially with regard to his imminent return doctrine.

Continuing the timeline of Darby's hokey hermeneutics, we come to James H. Brookes, Presbyterian pastor of two large churches in St. Louis, Missouri from 1864 to 1897. His teaching, combining the Covenant Theology of John Calvin with the replacement theology of earlier theologians, drew upon the Brethren's and therefore Darby's clear-cut distinction between Israel and the Church.

Brookes' monthly periodical The Truth regularly carried articles by Brethren members like H.H. Snell, William Lincoln and others. He also often recommended the writings of Brethren authors, making it likely that much of his dispensational teaching was derived from Darby and his followers in the Brethren.

Brookes was instrumental in furthering the spread of Darby's new method of interpretation. One of the organizers of the interdenominational Niagara Bible Conference in 1878, he served as its president from the time of its inception until his death in 1897. The Conference regularly hosted teachers and preachers who taught the dispensational message until its dissolution in 1990.

Contemporary evangelical critics of the teaching pointed to the Brethren as the source of the errant doctrine, challenging the spurious scholarship of its proponents. Of course Brookes and his fellow dispensationalists took umbrage at the suggestion that their beliefs might be in error. Who doesn't take offense at being told they're wrong? However, the height of folly is to cling to error in the face of clear evidence to the contrary, which is the course Brookes chose.

In attempting to refute his detractors, Brookes appealed to the aforementioned arguments between Darby and Newton, both of whom were Brethren members, to substantiate the validity of Dispensational interpretation. He incorrectly attributes the premillennial/post tribulation doctrine to Newton, accusing any who differed with the Dispensational teaching of having a shallow mind. In his words: *"They claim that (the pre-tribulation rapture) is the Plymouth Brethren view, and, owing to the universal detestation with which this sect is held by all other sects, they use the argument with powerful effect on many shallow minds. But they forget that their own view is Plymouth Brethrenism. J. N. Darby and B. W. Newton had a quarrel more than fifty years ago, the latter a very able and scholarly man, becoming the founder of the doctrine that the church will pass through the tribulation.'*[88]

Claiming that Newton was the originator of the post-tribulation doctrine is a specious argument at best, as a brief study of the teachings of the Early Church Fathers will reveal. I make a distinction between Early Church Fathers and those the Church typically appeal to for doctrinal justification, i.e. Justin Martyr, Augustine and other theologians of the 3rd and 4th centuries. The direct disciples of John the Apostle and their disciples, like Irenaeus and Hippolytus, give a much clearer picture of what was taught and believed in the early Church. Their teaching was decidedly pre-millenial/post tribulational, much as modern Christianity might decry otherwise.

Darby's dispensational teaching with its attendant imminent return doctrine came under increasing scrutiny after the death of Brookes in 1897 and the disbanding of the Niagara Bible Conference in 1900. Many of the original founders of the Conference who were still alive at the time of Brookes' death had already left the Conference. The reason most gave was that they could not continue believing a doctrine for which they could find no evidence in Scripture. They had changed their views on the any moment pre-tribulation Rapture of the saints.

One would think with the demise of the most effective disseminator of Darby's Dispensational Doctrine the new teaching would fade into obscurity. One would think wrong. Enter Arno C. Gaebelein.

The year following the dissolution of the Niagara Bible Conference, Gaebelein announced the formation of the Seacliff Bible Conference. In a bold stroke of Nicolaitan control, he ensured that the imminent return pre-

---

[88] James H. Brookes, "Who Shall Be Caught Up?" Volume XX The Truth, April 1894, p. 204

tribulation rapture doctrine would continue to propagate by only allowing teachers who upheld the teaching to speak at the conference.

Gaebelein immigrated to America from Germany in 1897 and became a Methodist minister in New York City. Coming under the influence of several Brethren members, he was soon convinced of the imminent return doctrine and became a fierce defender and promoter of what Darby and his followers taught concerning the future of the Jews and the Church.

Adopting Darby's dispensational views, Gaebelein left the Methodist denomination and set about spreading the doctrine throughout the Church through his newly formed Seacliff Bible Conference. His beliefs were clearly the result of exposure to Brethren teachings as the following quote shows:

> *"Through these brethren beloved, I had become acquainted with the work of those able and godly men who were used in the great spiritual movement of Brethren in the early part of the nineteenth century, John Nelson Darby and others. I found in his writings, in the works of William Kelly, McIntosh, F.W. Grant, Bellet and others the sould food I needed. I esteem these men next to the Apostles in their sound and spiritual teaching."*[89]

A regular speaker on the Bible conference circuit and highly respected teacher at the Seacliff Bible Conference was an individual who is probably hands down the one most responsible in history for the explosive dissemination throughout the Church of Darby's dispensational teaching.

When Cyrus Ingersoll Scofield approached Gaebelein with the idea of publishing a dispensational Bible, he was met with overwhelming approval. Gaebelein was so on board with the idea that he responded with, to use a vernacular, "I got a guy"; he indeed had a couple of guys as a matter of fact. Two of the Brethren members who influenced him with Darby's doctrines happened to be wealthy businessmen in New York City who were more than happy to fund Scofield while he wrote his "Bible". I use quotes because the Scofield Study Bible is not a "Bible"; it's a commentary on the Bible; and an extremely biased one at that.

C.I. Scofield

---

[89] A. C. Gaebelein, Half a Century, "Our Hope," 1930, pp. 84–85

Cyrus Ingerson Scofield grew up in Tennessee where he served as a soldier in the Confederate Army during the Civil War. After the war, he studied law in St. Louis, Missouri. He served as a state legislator in Kansas for a number of years after being admitted to the bar in that state. After a short stint as U.S. Attorney, he returned to St. Louis to practice law. It was also there that he met James H. Brookes, who commenced to teaching him everything he knew about Darby's method of prophetic interpretation.

By the time Darby died in 1882, Scofield had been fully groomed to take on the mantle of dispensational and "any-moment" dogmas bequeathed to him by his doctrinal predecessors. From that year until 1885, he served as pastor of a Congregational church in Dallas, Texas, which gave him fertile ground to plant the seeds of Darby doctrine in preaching from the pulpit and in regular Bible studies. From there, Scofield did a twelve year pastoral stint with the Congregational Church of East Northfield, Massachusetts.

With the financial backing of the aforesaid New York businessmen, Scofield was free to work on his commentary unimpeded by ordinary daily necessities. Loathe to call his opus a commentary, it was named The Scofield Reference Bible, and after its release in 1909 became a sensational best seller over the next few decades. It is undoubtedly the single greatest influence in Christianity's acceptance of dispensational and pre-tribulation rapture dogma.

Not only were Darby's commentaries flying off the shelves of book stores, they were strategically placed in Bible colleges and seminaries around the country. That meant thousands of Evangelists, Pastors and other Bible Teachers hit the ground running so to speak, teaching and preaching Darby Doctrine alongside the Gospel message right out of the chute. The natural assumption would be made that because of the incredible revivals and spiritual renewals that were taking place under their ministries, they had God's stamp of approval on all they taught and believed. That assumption doesn't hold water in light of the fact that many Evangelists and Bible Teachers held beliefs that were contrary to Darby's yet experienced the same astounding results.

Few Dispensationalists then or now take the time to prove whether the doctrine was taught in the early Church or if it was a latter day interpretation. A quick review of the words of Hippolytus and Irenaeus will

115

show the former to be the case. Fewer still will take the time to seek the truth concerning what was taught in the early Church about the Antichrist. Most theologians quote the Church Fathers, to whom I say, go back; back before Augustine; before Justin Martyr. Go back to the earliest Church Fathers, those who were taught by the Apostle John and his direct disciples. Those leaders of the Early Church tell us the Church must endure the persecution of the Antichrist during the Tribulation. They say true Believers will be rescued only when Jesus Christ returns in the clouds of glory to destroy the Antichrist. Early Church Fathers tell us is obvious when you consider the fact that Irenæus taught Hippolytus things he learned from men who studied under the Apostle John. He says those men told him John had taught them things he heard Jesus Christ Himself teach. So one must either believe what Irenæus and these other men said or else call them liars. I see no reason to do the latter. Therefore, I am left with the conclusion that what they say must be true.

How is it that a Bible teacher can have such a powerful effect if their message is mixed with error? Quite simply, in the words of the Bard, *"Gold is still gold whether in a thieves' or a fool's pocket."* With apologies to him, it might be said this way *"Truth is still truth, whether in a liar's or a deceiver's mouth."* The Word of God will not return to Him void, but will accomplish what He sent it to do, no matter how much garbage the Enemy tries to mix into it. There is power in the Word of God; power to change lives, to bring hope to the hopeless and help to the helpless. The devil knows that. It's the reason his lies are couched in layers of truth. In Satan's failed bid to tempt Jesus in the wilderness, he quoted Scripture, albeit misapplied and out of context.

You can bet misuse of Truth will be his most powerful weapon in the coming end time deception that promises to dwarf anything he's ever accomplished through all of history, rivaling the first deceit in the Garden of Eden, all based upon that very same lie. Hath God said? Did God really say or is that just a misunderstanding? Did God say His law was eternal, or should we understand that to mean it's eternal until Jesus comes? Or is it only eternal for Jews who have no better sense than to try to keep an unkeepable law? The inevitable consequence of admixture of truth and error however is damaging to the Gospel message, causing confusion and division, thwarting or at least diminishing in no small part our call to be a light to the nations.

Rest assured, no minister of the Gospel will be held blameless at the Judgment Seat for failing to prove for himself the veracity of another man's doctrines before adopting it as his own. Teachers are held to a higher standard and those of us who have influence over other believers should do so with fear and trembling. As a teacher, nothing causes me more angst than to think I have misled God's children with twisted teaching of His Word.

All of life is a test and as I approach my turn at the final exam, I cannot in good conscience leave this earthly life knowing I did not do and say everything in my power to warn believers and nonbelievers alike. Like the tin can robot in the 1960s scifi series Lost in Space repeatedly warned its intractable charge "Danger! Danger, Will Robinson!" I'm saying danger! Danger, Church of the living God! The Antichrist is on the horizon and the only way to escape the incredible catastrophe of the coming deception that is even now enveloping the whole world is to know the truth. Not cunningly devised fables about the truth, but knowing truth alone is what sets the captives free.

When Satan appears as the Antichrist Christians, Jews, atheists, politicians, all will potentially come under his spell of deception. What you choose to do with the Truth is entirely up to you. However, if you haven't already thrown this book across the room and rejected its message, you need to realize that none of us is immune from his deceptive wiles. As I warned you at the outset, if you have never considered the possibility that Satan might already have you believing his lies, you should begin now. Peter did not call Satan "the Adversary" (1 Pet. 5:8) for no good reason. The primary target of Satan's unrelenting attention is, and always has been, anyone who seeks to know the truth and follow God's will. That is, Satan is constantly standing against all who have experienced the new birth. Immediately after a person has heard the Truth concerning God's plan of salvation and has responded to it in the way that God requires, Satan attacks, using the arsenal of lies he has instilled in society over the years. His goal is always the same: get the true believer to deny some essential truth he has already believed. If you were not aware of that, the chances are Satan has already deceived you in a variety of ways. Satan has several extremely convincing lies at his disposal today. You are likely to hear one or more of them preached from the pulpit on any given Sunday. I hear them on the television and radio all the time. For example, one of Satan's most insidious lies repeated ad infinitum is that the Law has been done away with, relegated to another time and another people, replaced by Grace. With deft sleight of hand that would be the envy of any stage magician, he sprinkles enough truth into the lie to make the falsehood palatable to an amazing number of Christians today.

Sadly, when it comes to the attitude of some when confronted with challenges to their learned interpretations, they don't really want the truth. They just want constant reassurance that what they believe is the truth.

9
BUT PAUL SAID ...

Boy, if I had a nickel for every time I've heard that ...

Paul is the favorite apostle of Christians to quote when proving the abolition of the law, mostly because he's so easily misunderstood and therefore misinterpreted, exactly as Peter said he would be.[90] Just to clear the air and see what exactly Paul did say and not what so and so told so and so that so and so said that Paul said, we'll start with a well-known statement found in millions of Bibles around the world.

The Two Systems, Law and Grace, Cannot Co-Exist

--Schofield Reference Bible, pg. 1269 subheading, Galatians chapter 4

The principle expressed in that phrase has become a major tenet of modern Christianity. Clearly an outgrowth of the replacement and dispensational theologies discussed earlier, the inseparable river of Divine revelation is forced into an interpretation that divides two eternal concepts into polar opposites, pitting one against the other with an either/or conclusion, black/white, one or the other.

---

[90] 2Pe 3:16 As also in all his epistles, speaking in them of these things; in which are some things hard to be understood, which they that are unlearned and unstable wrest, as they do also the other scriptures, unto their own destruction.

119

When the eternal Word of God is reduced to a set of systems, truth is easily manipulated to say whatever one wants to make it say. When we elevate men's interpretation of Scripture to the level of God's Word and build our doctrines on those personal interpretations, we do exactly what Jesus rebuked the Pharisees for doing. He called them hypocrites, a den of vipers, sepulchers full of dead men's bones. Does this mean Yeshua was against them for keeping Torah? Of course not! It was because they were **not** keeping Torah but making the Commandments of God of none effect by the traditions of men.[91] He rebukes the religious leaders not for **keeping** the law, but for **not** keeping the law while strangling the life out of God's people with their manmade laws and traditions.[92] Notice he didn't chastise them for keeping certain of the Commandments; it was just that they were leaving out the weightier matters.

One can imagine Paul's horror at hearing how his words have been twisted in today's Christian theology. He might say *"I know that you believe you understand what you think I said, but I'm not sure you realize that what you heard is not what I meant."*[93]

Did Paul really say that law and grace can't co-exist? He did not! Cyrus Ingersoll Schofield said law and grace cannot co-exist. Then why do we attach divine authority to a subheading that is completely antithetical to other of Paul's writing?

It is difficult to believe the same Paul that supposedly preached the abolition of the law out of one side of his mouth declared out of the other to Timothy that **all Scripture** was sufficient for salvation, correct doctrine, for instruction in righteous behavior, able to equip one for all good works.[94] Yet that is precisely what modern Christianity teaches, that Paul was given a

---

[91] Mar 7:13 Making the word of God of none effect through your tradition, which ye have delivered: and many such like things do ye.

[92] Mat 23:23 Woe unto you, scribes and Pharisees, hypocrites! for ye pay tithe of mint and anise and cummin, and have omitted the weightier matters of the law, judgment, mercy, and faith: these ought ye to have done, and not to leave the other undone.

[93] Robert McCloskey quote from thinkexist.com

[94] 2Ti 3:15-17 And that from a child thou hast known the holy scriptures, which are able to make thee wise unto salvation through faith which is in Christ Jesus. All scripture is given by inspiration of God, and is profitable for doctrine, for reproof, for correction, for instruction in righteousness: That the man of God may be perfect, thoroughly furnished unto all good works.

divine mandate with authority to change what God had declared and expected of his people from the very beginning. If so, Paul was either confused, schizophrenic, deluded, a blatant liar **or** he has been misinterpreted just as Peter said he would be, by those who don't rightly understand the rest of Scripture. [Author's note: the only Scripture in existence at the time was the Old Testament.]

This is a clear warning given to the assembly about Paul's writings for those who pervert his teachings, which Peter says leads to their own destruction. Yet modern Christianity teaches a corrupted interpretation of Paul's writing, regardless of whether or not it fits with other verses in the Scriptures, even of Paul's own writing.

Using Paul's words, or a twisted interpretation of his words, the Church teaches we have been freed from the bondage of God's Law/Commandments. We're taught to think and act accordingly. Friends, even if Paul did teach abolition of the law, when it's all said and done we're called to be disciples of Jesus, not of Paul or Apollos or your pastor or anyone else for that matter. Paul said to follow him as he followed Christ. If you are following a perverted image of Paul that contradicts Jesus' teachings in any way, you are not following the Jesus of the Bible.

The Gospel, the Whole Gospel and Nothing but the Gospel

To be clear the gospel message, the whole counsel of God, is comprised of the entirety of Scripture from Genesis to Revelation. All of the types and antitypes, the feasts, allegories and indeed every word of Scripture point to the singular most important event of history, either predictively or in retrospect, the culmination of God's plan of salvation for mankind. Anointed eyes will see Christ crucified, buried, resurrected and ascended according to all that was written in the Torah, the prophets and the writings, and most certainly in the Apostolic Writings from Matthew to Revelation. The Jewish sages taught that when Messiah comes he would interpret even the spaces between the letters. He did exactly that while He walked on the earth. He said time and again *"You've heard it said"* or *"It is written"* with a caveat: *"But I say to you"*. In other words, Jesus was saying it's one thing to know the letter of the law but quite another to know the spirit of the law. He rightly interpreted the law in its spiritual reality, or in Biblical parlance, fulfilled the law.

The gospel message is one of grace and all that issues from it; forgiveness, salvation, justification, sanctification, faith, eternal life and power to live an overcoming life in this world. But that is only one side of the coin, or one side of the two-edged sword, as it were. The other side is one of justice, authority, holiness, and an expectation of expressed righteousness in obedience to the Lordship of Jesus Christ. The sword of the Spirit cuts through all religious pretenses, man-made commandments, church dogma and artificial divisions, revealing the pure unadulterated Revelation of the Mind of God if we'll just let Scripture mean what it says. Anything else is another Gospel, another Jesus.

The foundation of Jewish thought and belief, iterated by Jesus[95] when asked about the greatest commandment is what is called the *shema* in Deuteronomy 6:4 *"Hear O Israel. YHWH our God YHWH is ONE"*. We have **one** God, not an Old Testament God and a New Testament God; with **one** plan to redeem His people, not plan A with a backup plan B due to the failure of His chosen people to keep plan A; **one** undivided stream of revelation, not a polarized tome that pits one eternal truth against another; **one** people of God, made up of all believers from Adam to the last person at the Great White Throne, not two people with two distinct eternal fulfillments.[96]

What Paul Really Said

Before tackling a few of the misinterpretations of the *but Paul said* crowd, let's look at what he really did say. Following is a list of quotes by and about the Church's favorite alleged antinomian with commentary in brackets.

1. Paul was a Jew (Acts 21:39) and a Pharisee (Acts 26:5)
2. Paul's message did not contradict the Old Testament. The Bereans examined the Scriptures daily whether what he said was true. (Acts 17:11) [They tested his teachings against the Old Testament]
3. Paul's custom was to go to synagogue on the Sabbath. (Acts 13:14,42,44, 17:2, 18:4)
4. He was accused of teaching against God's Law (Acts 21:21) [He defended against those claims, insisting he was faithful to Torah]

---

[95] Mat 22:37 Jesus said unto him, Thou shalt love the Lord thy God with all thy heart, and with all thy soul, and with all thy mind.

[96] Eph 4:4-6 There is one body, and one Spirit, even as ye are called in one hope of your calling; One Lord, one faith, one baptism, One God and Father of all, who is above all, and through all, and in you all.

5. His accusers had no proof that he broke any of God's Laws (Acts 24:13,14) [On the contrary, he defended himself saying he believed all that was written in the Law and the Prophets]

6. Paul kept the law and instructed others to do the same (Acts 21:24)

7. Paul said Ananias was a devout man because he kept God's Law (Acts 22:12)

8. He said the law is not made void by faith, but that we establish the law (Rom 3: 31)

9. He said the law is not sin, but by it comes the knowledge of sin (Rom 7:7)

10. He said the law and the Commandments are holy, righteous and good (Rom 7:12,16)

11. He said the law is not what leads us to death (Rom 7:13) [Breaking the law leads to death]

12. He said he delights in God's law (Rom 7:22) [See also Ps. 40:8]

13. He said He serves the law of God with his mind but his flesh serves the law of sin (Rom 7:25)

14. He said the law is good, and that one must use it properly. (1Tim 1:8) [Misuse of the Law is to look to law as the means of salvation]

15. Paul said all Scripture is God-breathed and is intended for teaching, rebuking, correcting and training in righteousness. 2 Timothy 3:16-17 [In other words, everything Christianity claims as New Testament doctrine is found in the Old Testament, the foundation of the New]

16. Paul made the trip to Jerusalem to celebrate the Feasts according to the law (Acts 18:21; 20:16; Ex. 34:22; Lev 23)

17. Paul appealed to the law in defense against those who abused the law against him. (Acts 23:3) [If Paul supposedly taught the law was abolished, how could he rightly use the law to defend himself?]

18. Paul taught keeping of the Passover (1Cor 5:8)

19. Paul quotes Deut 27:26 – a person breaking God's law is cursed (Gal 3:10)

20. Paul quotes Hab 2:4 – the just shall live by faith (Gal 3:11)

21. Paul quotes Lev 18:5 – the man who keeps God's law, lives because of it (Gal 3:12)

22. Paul quotes Deut 11:26-28 & 27:15-26 – the curses of the law (Gal 3:13)

23. Paul quotes Lev 19:18 – Love thy neighbor as thy self (Gal 5:14)

24. Paul quotes Deut 5:16 – Honor thy father and mother (Eph 6:2)

Despite these clear statements, some will still say he kept the law because he was a Jew, and that we don't have to since the law was given to the Jews. Friends, you've been lied to. The Liar convinced the Church with the same lie he spoke to Eve: *"hath God said"*, the same lie he whispers in your ear right this minute. Did God really mean His law was eternal, immutable, meant for all His people of all times, or was the law really just one of several tests meant for another people of another time, only to be discarded when it outlived its usefulness?

First of all, the law was given to all of Israel. Second, standing with all the tribes of Israel at the foot of Mt. Sinai was a mixed multitude of peoples who came out of Egypt with them during the Exodus. Third, the law was intended for the native-born Israelite as well as the foreigners in their midst who had accepted the God of Israel (Ex. 12:49; Lev. 24:22; Num. 15:15, 16). Fourth, Paul said there is no more Jew & Gentile (Gal 3:28). Fifth, Jesus said there is only one flock (John 10:16). Sixth, we are now grafted into Israel (Rom 11:16-26); and prior to becoming partakers of the covenant of promise, we were Gentiles [past tense], aliens from the commonwealth of Israel and without God in the world (Eph. 2:11-13).

Poor Paul, the Least in the Kingdom of Heaven

If Paul really does teach us to forsake the law, then according to the words of the Master[97], the place reserved for him in the Kingdom is somewhere far back at the end of the line. The prevalent understanding of Paul's words has him breaking almost all of God's commandments as well as teaching others that the law is no longer applicable. If so, according to Christ's own words, Paul would be the least in the Kingdom of Heaven. How can Paul go against God's words which clearly states no one can add to or abolish any of God's Commandments (Deut 4:2, 12:32) and (Rev. 22:18, 19)?

That said it seems anytime one makes reference to the law, sin, conviction and repentance alongside grace in certain circles, icicles begin to form in the atmosphere. Discussing these terms usually causes an immediate cognitive

---

[97] Mat 5:19 Whosoever therefore shall break one of these least commandments, and shall teach men so, he shall be called the least in the kingdom of heaven: but whosoever shall do and teach them, the same shall be called great in the kingdom of heaven.

The view that Christians are released by grace from the obligation of observing the moral law.

"anti-law" Greek

disconnect as they have become so distorted by the toxic "antinomian" theology ingrained in the historical Church. Most people turn a deaf ear to any discussion that might contradict what they've already accepted and so much of what is accepted is derived from early Church theologians whose interpretations bent toward the will of the Roman Catholic Church, not from Scripture itself.

Focusing solely on the grace of God without preaching the divine law, justice and judgment of God is unbalanced. Remember, John 3:16 doesn't just tell us that God loved us and gave his son for us. It also tells us we will perish unless we receive the substitutionary atonement of Jesus.

There is a phrase in financial circles that says *"When America sneezes, the whole world catches cold",* meaning that because of the global status of the US dollar as the world's reserve currency, if the US markets hiccup, the whole world suffers financially. On a spiritual level, it seems the US has created a culture in which God's law is physically removed from public view across the nation, from public schools first, then from the courts of judgment. Why? Quite simply, it was spiritually removed from churches first. We as a nation then exported that lawless doctrinal bias to the rest of the world in the name of evangelism. And the whole Christian world caught a spiritual cold. What a shame! Just as the global dominance of the US dollar is eroding, so is the dominance of lawless doctrine in the Church seeing an erosion of its deleterious effects in the Church at large.

King David wrote, "*I am a stranger on earth; do not hide your commands from me. My soul is consumed with longing for your laws at all times*"-- Ps. 119:19 and in Ps. 40:8 *"I delight to do thy will, O my God; Thy law is within my heart".* Taking delight in God's law today may place one squarely in the crosshairs of those who are zealous anti-law defenders of Grace, a stranger indeed. Messages of lawlessness, disguised as grace, abound within the body of Christ in these last days. [Typically, any discussion of God's law is immediately deemed legalistic and anti-grace, part of the *Old Testament* rules and regulations.] Many Christians are so completely influenced by the anti-law doctrine that anytime someone preaches a message that sounds like law they become angry and instantly tune it out.

As the hyper-grace message has become the predisposition in today's church culture, have we become unbalanced? Is there a place in our preaching to present law alongside grace? Is it possible under the New Covenant to once again take delight in the law of God? Bear with me as I ask a few of these important questions and pray the Holy Spirit sheds light on our pursuit of truth.

Paul the Apostle in no way diminishes Torah while preaching Jesus Christ, but he frequently uses two idiomatic expressions, **works of the law** and **under the law**, both of which lend themselves to an antinomian (anti-law) interpretation if one is pre-disposed to believe the Old Testament law has been done away with.

These phrases were used to expose false religion, not to teach abolition of Torah. Paul alluded to other designations of law with phrases like *Law of Sin and Death* and *Law of Life*[98]. Not to be outdone, James speaks of the *Law of Liberty*[99].

Paul distinguished between these uses of law and God's law, but we will only see that when we accept that he and all the other first century believers held to Torah while rejecting un-Biblical traditions. It explains how the *law* can be Holy on the one hand, while the *law* can be a yoke of bondage on the other. It's not the same law! Making Paul teach certain things contrary to the clear words of Jesus and the writers of the Old Testament forces us to interpret his words to fit what we already believe rather than in a way that is consistent with **all scripture**.

We hear many well-meaning Christian Pastors, Teachers or Evangelists talk about how Christian faith is diametrically opposed to the law; that grace is unmerited favor [true], but that grace is the opposite of and contradictory to the law [false]. Most do not take the time to consider that the other side of grace is pardon, an integral aspect of the law. It has long amazed me how a preacher can deliver a wonderful sermon on Ephesians 2:8, 9 and invariably ignore verse ten-"*for we are his workmanship, created in Christ Jesus unto good works, which God hath before ordained that we should walk in them*"-a most critical part of the context of that passage.

These two terms *"Works of the Law"* and *"Under the Law"* have been very poorly interpreted and are being taught erroneously in most Christian and even many Messianic settings today. These two terms if understood as Paul

---

[98] Rom 8:2 For the law of the Spirit of life in Christ Jesus hath made me free from the law of sin and death.
[99] Jas 1:25 But whoso looketh into the perfect law of liberty, and continueth therein, he being not a forgetful hearer, but a doer of the work, this man shall be blessed in his deed.

intended, have the potential to greatly transform our understanding of Paul and his teaching based on what he said, not on what we think he said. Rightly dividing Paul's words potentially brings far greater understanding of the Messiah and the anointing of the Holy Spirit in the Christian's life.

Legalism, Falling From Grace and the Judaizer

Before addressing those terms Paul did actually use, let us note some things that Paul did not say, yet are used by many NT believers as though they were the very Word of God.

Those who seek to adopt pursuance of the Torah into their walk with the Savior as the first century believers did are often labeled *legalists* and *Judaizers*. Those terms, while nowhere to be found in the Bible, do actually describe a serious flaw in fundamental doctrine if we place our faith of salvation in works based on their meanings.

Let's give proper definition of the terms so we're speaking the same language.

- **Legalism** - the idea that you can obey God's laws well enough that your own effort will save you.

- **Judaizer** – one who seeks to draw a believer away from a grace-centered salvation into a salvation based on law. (See above)

- **Fallen From Grace** – forsaking salvation by grace through faith in exchange for a works-based salvation. (Used by Paul to describe the above) Fallen from Grace is defined within the passage *"Christ is become of no effect unto you, whosoever of you are justified by the law; ye are fallen from grace."* Gal 5:4

All have sinned and come short of the glory of God. There is none righteous, no, not one. No amount of good works will ever merit salvation. One will never keep the laws well enough to be justified in the eyes of God. To fall into that doctrinal trap is to be in danger of hellfire. But there is another word that demands definition as well:

- **Licentious** - the idea that because of grace you have been set free from obeying His laws. From Dictionary.com: *"unrestrained by law or general morality; lawless; immoral."* Merriam/Webster defines it thus: 1) *"lacking legal or moral restraints; especially: disregarding sexual restraints 2) marked by disregard for strict rules of correctness"*

Jude, the brother of the Lord Jesus, warned of those who would pervert God's Grace and make it a doctrine of lawlessness. *"For there are certain men crept in unawares, who were before of old ordained to this condemnation, ungodly men, turning the grace of our God into lasciviousness, and denying the only Lord God, and our Lord Jesus Christ."* Jude 1:4

The 1828 edition of Webster's American Dictionary of the English Language defines the word thusly:

LICEN'TIOUS, a. [L. licentiosus.]

1. Using license; indulging freedom to excess; unrestrained by law or morality; loose; dissolute; as a licentious man.
2. Exceeding the limits of law or propriety; wanton; unrestrained; as licentious desires. Licentious thoughts precede licentious conduct.
LICEN'TIOUSLY, adv.
With excess of liberty; in contempt of law and morality.
LICEN'TIOUSNESS, n.
Excessive indulgence of liberty; contempt of the just restraints of law, morality and decorum. The licentiousness of authors is justly condemned; the licentiousness of the press is punishable by law.
          (1828 edition of Webster's American Dictionary of the English Language)

And from Black's Law Dictionary:

 LICENTIOUSNESS
The indulgence of the arbitrary will of the individual, without regard to ethics or law, or respect for the rights of others. In this it differs from "liberty;" for the latter term may properly be used only of the exercise of the will in its moral freedom, with justice to all men and obedience to the laws. Welch v. Duraiul, 30 Conn. 1S4, 4 Am. Rep. 55; State v. Brigman, 94 N. C. 8S9.

In a narrower and more technical sense, the word is equivalent to lewdness or lasciviousness. Holton v. State, 28 Fla. 303, 9 South. 710.

(Black's Law Dictionary)

Even the secular philosopher Plato understood the necessity for law in civilized society when he said "*Law is the god of wise men; licentiousness is the god of fools*".

Finally, lest one doubt the theology of lawlessness matches precisely with the number one characteristic of the one we call anti-Christ, The Lawless One, hear what the prophet Ezekiel says about the matter:

> "*Her priests have violated my law, and have profaned mine holy things: they have put no difference between the holy and profane, neither have they shewed difference between the unclean and the clean, and have hid their eyes from my sabbaths, and I am profaned among them.*" Ezekiel 22:26

Dear pastor, teacher, evangelist, or missionary, are you teaching God's people to discern the difference between what is holy and profane? Do you teach them to discern what is clean and what is unclean? Do you, in your role as a shepherd, teach them to turn their eyes from God's Sabbaths? Are you, by teaching that these things don't apply to the Christian, unwittingly profaning YHWH before them and teaching them to do likewise?

Why is it when one seeks to be obedient to Christ's call to love Him by keeping his commandments, a person is dismissed by misguided defenders of grace as trusting in works of the law or fallen from grace? Why is keeping His commandments purely as an act of love condemned as being legalistic?

We are justified by grace through faith. Period. Nothing we do can ever add to his matchless saving grace. Let us ask and answer this question - do we honestly believe that simply by attempting to obey God in keeping his laws as an expression of love and gratitude, that we are actually earning our salvation? If there is even a hint of self-worth in our doctrine, we have made the commandments of God of none effect. We have diminished the glory of his atoning sacrifice on our behalf. If we could gain any measure of salvation through our good works, then logically we could establish all our own righteousness. And if that was possible, the Savior's death on the cross was in vain. The rich typology presented in the sacrifices and myriad similitudes throughout the Old Testament would be nothing more than ritual borrowed from the pagan nations.

May it never be! We affirm emphatically that all our righteous deeds are as filthy rags in God's sight; that in reality we have no good works that commend us to salvation. Any and all righteousness we have is granted to us freely by God as a result of the death of His son on the cross and our acceptance of that free gift. It is only by His imputed righteousness that we may stand before the Holy One, forgiven, justified and born anew by His word. If we are drawn to express our gratitude by walking in obedience to His commandments, it is only because we have been empowered by the Holy Spirit to do so. Abraham believed God, and it was reckoned to him for righteousness. It was faith that justified Abraham, the Father of the faithful.[100] And it was faith that moved him to obedience in keeping God's law (Torah).[101]

Noah found grace in the eyes of God. Grace was acted upon by faith. Faith was demonstrated by obedience to God's instruction, and that obedience resulted in Noah and his family being saved from the destruction of the flood.

Indeed, all the Saints listed in the "Hall of Faith" (Heb. 11) walked by faith. And each one validated their faith in acts of righteousness, as is clearly shown in the first one listed, Abel:

> *"By faith Abel offered unto God a more excellent sacrifice than Cain, by which he obtained witness that he was righteous, God testifying of his gifts: and by it he being dead yet speaketh."* Heb 11:4

We may consider the demands of Jesus to keep his commandments as just nifty suggestions on how to be a better person. However, we might be better served to view them from His viewpoint, as an expression of love; as acts of obedience and rich gratitude for what he has so freely given by grace.

Here's the raw truth: no amount of obedience can save you, yet, without obedience you cannot be saved. Obeying the law doesn't save you. But not obeying the law is a sure sign saving grace has not found you. The law doesn't save you, it exposes you. And if you're saved, it reveals the Savior in you.

---

[100] Gal 3:7 Know ye therefore that they which are of faith, the same are the children of Abraham.
[101] Gen 26:5 Because that Abraham obeyed my voice, and kept my charge, my commandments, my statutes, and my laws.

Why? A changed heart is the result of grace. The evidence of a changed heart is a desire to walk in obedience to God. If no desire to obey is evident a change has not occurred. If we remain children of disobedience we remain outside the New Covenant. What is the New Covenant? Here it is in a nutshell:

> Jeremiah 31:33 "... *After those days, saith the* LORD, *I will put my* **law [Torah]** *in their inward parts, and write it in their hearts; and will be their God, and they shall be my people.*"

It is the Abrahamic Covenant in full bloom, fully realized in the Person of God's own son and made real in the lives of all who receive by faith the gift of salvation by grace. The New Covenant is the culmination of every promise of redemptive grace to every generation of fallen mankind since the first Adam bit into the lie of salvation by works. It is you; it is me; it is the unspeakable joy of knowing that a loving Creator had plans from the very beginning to pull us out of the quagmire of bondage to sin if we would just trust Him. And the evidence of that trust, the clear demonstration of the reality of that faith is simple childlike obedience to His Word. His Word is His law. His law is an expression of His divine will. His law and His will are inseparable. His law is rooted in the essence of His being. In the essence of His character He is righteous. So if the commandments are given by God to His people, then they are founded in His righteous character. He would not demand something of His people that is not righteous. His laws are a reflection of His character. We reflect His righteous character when we respond by faith in obedience.

Obedience to what, one might ask? To some vague concept to love God and love your fellow man? As the song says, is that all there is? Or does God give us an instruction manual that spells out how we are to love God and love our fellow man? Are there practical instructions on how to keep the motor running smoothly; when to check the oil, balance the tires and do regular maintenance? Why yes, there is such a manual. It's your Bible, the totality of God's Word from Genesis to Revelation.

Those with an ear to hear will hear echoes of Torah when they read the New Testament. From the Gospels to the letters of Paul, John and the others, all are rooted and grounded in the Old Testament. The Torah was never about strict adherence to a set of precepts and impossible to keep commandments. It was always about teaching us to love God with all our heart and to love our fellow man, with clear instructions on how to go about doing that. Torah in the beginning is the same refreshing water of life as it is at the end, where Paul expounds on the development of one's character as a result of walking in the Spirit.

What does that mean, to walk in the Spirit? Does that mean we toss out the textbook that our Tutor used to train us up in how we should go? Do we neglect and even impugn His instruction manual in favor of some nebulous, indefinable concept of love with no concrete instructions on its practical application? Friends, the Holy Spirit will never ever say anything contrary to what is already written. I submit that any spirit that teaches such is not the Holy Spirit of the living God but is the spirit of the Lawless One, another spirit and another gospel.

A believer's character is not mere moral or legal correctness, but the possession and manifestation of nine graces[102], all of which are well defined in the Torah.

> Love – Joy - Peace -- character as an inward state;

> Longsuffering – Gentleness - Goodness -- character in expression toward man;

> Faith – Meekness - Temperance -- character in expression toward God

Together, these character traits portray a moral portrait of Christ, defined by Paul's explanation of Gal. 2:20 *"Not I, but Christ ... "* and as a definition of *"fruit"* in John 15:1-8. This character is possible because of the vital union of the believer to the Creator, both before the crucifixion and after, i.e. John 15:5; 1 Cor. 12:12, 13; Lev. 19:18 and is wholly the fruit of the Spirit in those believers who are yielded to Him.

The word *torah* at its root doesn't mean "law". It means instruction, pointing the way like a teacher giving direction to a student or an archer aiming at the bullseye on a target. The purpose of Torah is not now and never was intended as a means of salvation. It is an instruction manual that defines the rules of the house! It describes how His children are expected to behave within the Household of God, having been adopted and granted all rights, benefits and privileges of a natural born child. The Scriptures teach

---

[102] Gal 5:22 But the fruit of the Spirit is love, joy, peace, longsuffering, gentleness, goodness, faith,
Gal 5:23 Meekness, temperance: against such there is no law.

us it is given to man as a picture of God's character, and seeing Him as He is, we are drawn to be like Him. The more clearly we see the beauty of His holiness the more we are drawn to be conformed to that image. Torah is an invitation to relationship with God. It is instruction about who He is and how we are to conduct our lives in a way that reflects His righteous behavior. Torah, both New Testament and Old, teaches us to put feet to our faith.

So the question is not *"Do I have to obey Torah?"* If Torah reveals the character of God and is an invitation for us to see Him, to love Him, to emulate Him, to want to be like Him, the question becomes, *"How do I live out Torah in my life in a way that practically demonstrates the reality of that relationship to the world around me?"*

Do you feed the hungry? That's Torah. Do you clothe the naked? That's Torah. Do you heal the sick, give hope to the hopeless, show the blind man the way and give a cup of cold water in His name? That's Torah manifest in the character of the individual who has been changed from the inside out to reflect God in the earth.

Many accept the invitation to a relationship with the Messiah of Torah but treat the Torah of Messiah with utter disdain. According to the Bible Jesus is the Torah made flesh, the Living Word. Sadly, many reject the invitation to a deeper relationship that comes through knowledge of the Written Word, God's instructions in righteousness to His people.

James, the brother of Jesus who penned the letter that bears his name, expounds on the inextricable connection between works and faith.[103] In other words, he's saying if you don't show fruit of true repentance in works of righteousness, he questions the validity of your claims to Biblical salvation. Faith is not passive. Faith is an action word. True faith is an active force imbued from the Author and Finisher of our faith that results in works of righteousness, not to be confused with *works of the law* in the sense that term is typically understood, as we'll show.

In a very simplistic way - don't you love how Truth really isn't all that complex? - I would summarize the idea like this: if you have truly found grace in the eyes of God, your faith will be validated by your faithfulness. Say that again with me: my faith is validated by my faithfulness. By it I

---

[103] Jas 2:18 Yea, a man may say, Thou hast faith, and I have works: shew me thy faith without thy works, and I will shew thee my faith by my works.

obtain witness of righteousness, just like Abel and all the other aforementioned heroes of faith.

"Man does not live by bread alone, but man lives by every word that comes from the mouth of YHWH." Deuteronomy 8:3

His Word tells us what pleases Him. How can we, His children, do any less than learn to do those things that please Him?

Works of the Law

The phrase *"works of the law"* is used six times in Paul's letters, listed here:

> Romans 3:28
>
> Romans 9:32
>
> Galatians 2:16
>
> Galatians 3:2
>
> Galatians 3:5
>
> Galatians 3:10

In each case the same Greek words are used, defined below:

> ϱγον ergon er'-gon from ἔϱγω ergō (a primary but obsolete word; to work); toil (as an effort or occupation); by implication an act: - deed, doing, labour, work.

> νόμος nomos nom'-os from a primary word νέμω nemō (to parcel out, especially food or grazing to animals); law (through the idea of prescriptive usage), generally (regulation), specifically (of Moses [including the volume]; also of the Gospel), or figuratively (a principle): - law.

Entire books are available that discuss in depth the meaning of this phrase, which we'll not attempt to duplicate in this short missive. We will comment however on the clear contextual intent of the author when Paul the Apostle used the terms.

In every case, the phrase is cast in a negative light. Those who interpret the passages with an anti-law bias will focus on the law as the culprit, when rightfully it is the *works of the law as a means of salvation* that is in question. Paul's emphasis is on the fact that salvation comes by faith, not by keeping the law in an effort to establish righteous standing before God. The focus is not on law per se. Rather it is on faith as the basis for salvation. Paul is in no way abrogating the law. He is simply drawing the distinction between true salvation that comes by faith as opposed to doing the works of the law as a means of justification.

A clear example of the misguided focus on law as the "bad guy" is seen in the treatment by much of Christianity of Gal. 3:10-13.

> *"For as many as are of the works of the law are under the curse: for it is written, Cursed is every one that continueth not in all things which are written in the book of the law to do them. But that no man is justified by the law in the sight of God, it is evident: for, The just shall live by faith. And the law is not of faith: but, The man that doeth them shall live in them. Christ hath redeemed us from the curse of the law, being made a curse for us: for it is written, Cursed is every one that hangeth on a tree:"*

To many Christian teachers, Paul is saying the law is the curse. However, that would clearly contradict what he wrote in Romans 3:31 and many other verses:

> *"Do we then make void the law through faith? God forbid: yea, we establish the law."*

How can Paul mean on the one hand that the law is cursed and on the other that the law is established by faith? Here again we see a system of hermeneutics that insists on an either/or interpretation; it's either works or faith, when in reality both have a part to play in a believer's salvation. Our faith is not in the law. Our faith is in God alone. And ours should be a faith that touches us, that moves us, draws us to walk[104] in the good works that we were created to do.

---

[104] Eph 2:10 For we are his workmanship, created in Christ Jesus unto good works, which God hath before ordained that we should walk in them.

The law is not the curse. The curse is the consequence of breaking the law; breaking the law results in being cursed. Clearly Paul is drawing a distinction between *works of the law* as a means of salvation and faith as the only acceptable means. The problem is not the law; the problem is trying to keep the law for one's salvation. Paul is saying if one is disposed to keeping the law for his salvation, then that one must keep all of the law perfectly, an impossible endeavor.

There are many words that describe different aspects of law in Hebrew. Paul, being Jewish, understood the distinctions. However the single Greek word νόμος *nomos* is used to translate all the various Hebrew terms in the New Testament. How unfortunate in this case. Those who are predisposed to believe that it refers to the Old Testament Scriptures readily refer to these passages to prove that Torah and all Biblical laws, commandments, statutes and ordinances are abolished and replaced by a new law, a law of Grace, a law of love, a law that is separate and distinct from God's *old* laws.

While the word law is used in a multitude of New Testament verses, translating the Greek word *"nomos"* as *"law"* in every case is problematic. The same word is used to translate law whether it is the law of Moses, the law of God or the laws of man or presumably even the laws of nature. When the Bible says *"nomos"* in Greek, it could refer to several different concepts. A first century Hebrew audience would have been able to distinguish between their respective meanings.

As New Testament believers it is imperative that we understand the author's previous use of words and phrases in their original context and meanings. That means defining words and interpreting Scripture according to the dictionary of those words, the Old Testament. That's not a new concept. One of the first rules of Biblical hermeneutics taught in seminaries is the *"law of first mention"*; how a word is first used in Scripture sets the foundation of how the word is defined and how it is used in subsequent passages. It may even require that we study how words are used in their cultural historical context.

One word Paul uses that is invariably equated with law in the minds of those bent on proving the law is done away with is the word ordinances, found in the following verses:

> Eph 2:15 Having abolished in his flesh the enmity, *even* the law of
> commandments *contained* in ordinances; for to make in
> himself of twain one new man, *so* making peace;

Col 2:14 Blotting out the handwriting of ordinances that was against us, which was contrary to us, and took it out of the way, nailing it to his cross;

The antinomian bias of the translator is evident in the first verse with the addition of the word *even* as though to stress the phrase *the law of commandments*, the implication being that Christ's crucifixion abolished the law of commandments, ie the Torah or law. The italicization of the word *even* means it was not in the original text. Viewed from the right perspective clearly he is stating that first, it was the enmity, that which makes us an enemy of God that was abolished, not His commandments. His laws don't make us an enemy of God; breaking the laws makes us an enemy of God. Second, the enmity Paul refers to seems to be a specific law of commandments contained in certain ordinances. Knowing what those ordinances are is critical to right understanding of these passages.

The verse in Colossians also uses the Greek word translated ordinance. Again, a mindset predisposed to see abolishment of law or Torah in Paul's writing sees that passage saying *"the law was nailed to the cross"*. But is that what Paul is saying?

First Paul uses a word that says whatever is against us, the thing that makes us enemies of God is obliterated, destroyed, erased, caused to cease having any power over our lives, translated *"blotting out"*; [Definitions from Strong's Concordance]

ἐξαλείφω, exaleiphō, ex-al-i'-fo, from G1537 and G218; to smear out, that is, obliterate (erase tears, figuratively pardon sin): - blot out, wipe away.

He then tells us what that thing is that was blotted out, *"the handwriting"*.

χειρόγραφον

cheirographon

khi-rog'-raf-on, neuter of a compound of G5495 and G1125; something hand written (chirograph), that is, a manuscript (specifically a legal document or bond (figuratively)): - handwriting.

Finally, the modifier of the subject, the *handwriting*, that is critical in properly exegeting this passage is the prepositional phrase *"of ordinances"*. So what Paul is saying is that a particular handwriting of ordinances that was against us was wiped out, erased, poof, gone like a vapor in the wind by the Lord's sacrifice on the cross.

Here is where an anti-law bias trips up most Christians in interpreting the verse. If those ordinances are assumed, as is the case with most Christian interpretations to be the Law, then the inescapable conclusion must be that Jesus's death on the cross did away with the law, seeing as how it was hung on the cross with Him and blotted out, right? If one is already convinced, that is exactly how the verse is interpreted. But let's see if that really is what Paul means. The word ordinance is translated from the Greek word

δόγμα

dogma

dog'-mah

From the base of G1380; a law (civil, ceremonial or ecclesiastical): - decree, ordinance.

What does dogma mean? From Merriam/Webster:

: a belief or set of beliefs that is accepted by the members of a group without being questioned or doubted

: a belief or set of beliefs that is taught by a religious organization

Further clarification comes from dictionary.com

1. *At the turn of the 17th century, dogma entered English from the Latin term meaning "philosophical tenet." The Greek word from which it is borrowed means "that which one thinks is true," and comes ultimately from the Greek dokeîn, which means "to seem good" or "think."* **The origin of the word dogma acts as a reminder to English speakers that now established principles and doctrines were once simply thoughts and opinions of ordinary people that gained popularity and eventually found their way into the universal consciousness of society.**

Twentieth-century American academic and aphorist Mason Cooley concisely observed that "Under attack, sentiments harden into dogma," *suggesting that dogma is spawned as a defensive act. This idea implies that for every dogma that exists, there is a counter dogma. With so many "truths" out there, there is sure to be a dogma to conveniently fit every set of beliefs; an official system of principles or tenets concerning faith, morals, behavior, etc., as of a church.* [Note: emphasis mine]

Synonyms: doctrine, teachings, set of beliefs, philosophy.

2. *a specific tenet or doctrine authoritatively laid down, as by a church: the dogma of the Assumption; the recently defined dogma of papal infallibility.*

Synonyms: tenet, canon, law.

3. *prescribed doctrine proclaimed as unquestionably true by a particular group:.*

Both ideas, dogma and Torah, are given equal footing in the common interpretations of most New Testament believers. In the minds of most translators, Torah equates to dogma equates to law. Given the careful use by Paul of specific words and their respective meanings, obviously this is an untenable position. To accept that position, a clear antinomian bias must be employed. The question must be asked: was Paul against Torah; legalism; dogma?

It was dogma that was nailed to the cross according to Paul. It was the decree that pronounced you and me guilty as charged. The wages of sin is death. All of mankind is without excuse and stands on the wrong side of the scales of justice with no means of escaping the death penalty. The handwriting blotted out was the bill of indictment against us, the guilty verdict that demanded death for breaking the law. It was blotted out, removed as an accusing witness against us by Christ wiping it out, taking it *"out of the way, and nailing it to his cross."* It was accomplished not by an arbitrary abolition of the Law. Moral failure cannot be removed in this manner. That can only be done by satisfying the just recompense for breaking the Law, the penalty which Christ accepted by his *"obedience unto death."* The decree of judgment was nailed to His cross. Those guilty parties who look to Him by faith are freed from the power of its condemnation.

It is one thing to consider Jesus taking our sins **upon** Himself. But the idea that He was *"made sin for us that we might be made the righteousness of God"* (2 Cor. 5:21) is nigh impossible to contemplate. Taking the place of our sin, He took the punishment that was due you and me. The handwriting, with the curse involved in it, was identified with him, and thus God condemned sin in Christ's flesh (Rom. 8:3). Christ exchanged places with us, cancelling the bill of indictment, the dogma, which named us in guilt and condemnation.

The document that declared you guilty of breaking the law and sentenced to die was nailed to the cross. When Jesus declared from the cross *"it is finished"*, He was saying this decree, the legal document that pronounces you guilty, the punishment which is death, is now paid in full.

The Greek word nomos can also mean legalism according to our previous definition of the word, or it can refer to dogma or even the sacrificial system. So a correct translation from the mindset of the authors would be *works of legalism*, trying to be saved by keeping laws. Lawlessness, the opposite side of the coin, is just as bad. Living by man's tradition instead of God's Commands is deadly regardless of what name it goes by or how sound the ecclesiological argument may seem.

Dead Works

Paul waged a ceaseless defense of the Gospel in opposition to the *works of the law* cult which demanded that one be circumcised and keep the Traditions of the Pharisees to be saved.

Throughout His ministry, Jesus warned the Jews that their genetic lineage had no bearing on whether a person is saved or not, saying:

> Mat 3:9, 10 *"And do not presume to say to yourselves, 'We have Abraham as our father,' for I tell you, God is able from these stones to raise up children for Abraham. Even now the axe is laid to the root of the trees. Every tree therefore that does not bear good fruit is cut down and thrown into the fire."*

Good fruit equates to good works. They are the same thing. He was telling the Pharisees to repent and show evidence of their repentance with good works as He says:

> Mat 3:8 *"Bear fruit in keeping with repentance."*

The good works being commanded here are in opposition to dead works, which many of the Jews of the time were guilty of. As the writer of the book of Hebrews says:

"Therefore let us leave the elementary doctrine of Christ and go on to maturity, not laying again a foundation of repentance from dead works and of faith toward God" Heb. 6:1

Dead works are those things that can be done for reasons other than faith toward God. And faith toward God is believing that he exists and that he will reward those who seek him. Just as the writer said in the same letter:

"And without faith it is impossible to please him, for whoever would draw near to God must believe that he exists and that he rewards those who seek him." Heb. 11:6

What kinds of things were done as dead works? A good deed done with the wrong motive is a dead work. The prophets may help us understand, as Isaiah says:

"What to me is the multitude of your sacrifices? says YHWH; I have had enough of burnt offerings of rams and the fat of well-fed beasts; I do not delight in the blood of bulls, or of lambs, or of goats. "When you come to appear before me, who has required of you this trampling of my courts? Bring no more vain offerings; incense is an abomination to me. New moon and Sabbath and the calling of convocations-- I cannot endure iniquity and solemn assembly. Your new moons and your appointed feasts my soul hates; they have become a burden to me; I am weary of bearing them. When you spread out your hands, I will hide my eyes from you; even though you make many prayers, I will not listen; your hands are full of blood." Isa 1:11-15

The offerings, sacrifices, and feasts were expressly commanded by God in the Torah. Why would God condemn something that He himself had required?

Doing the right thing the wrong way or with the wrong motive are met with severe consequences in Scripture. Examples: Uriah righted the Ark of the Covenant as it almost toppled from the wagon used to transport it and was struck dead. The Ark was not allowed to touch the ground and Uriah was simply trying to prevent that from happening. However, no one was allowed to touch the Ark, and Uriah paid the price for trespassing on holy ground.

Nadab and Abihu lit fire as the law commanded but with fire from a wrong source and were struck dead. The Commandment was for the priests to light the incense with fire taken from the burnt altar. They did the right thing but with strange fire and paid the price.

There is a way to approach the throne, and it is not with a brash or cavalier attitude. Yahweh exposes their hearts and tells them how to correct themselves, saying:

> "Wash yourselves; make yourselves clean; remove the evil of your deeds from before my eyes; cease to do evil, learn to do good; seek justice, correct oppression; bring justice to the fatherless, plead the widow's cause." Is. 1:16, 17

God sets before them good works as evidence of their repentance. Like any other Hebrew word, faith is an action word. The works required of them are a demonstration of faith that is validated by their faithfulness. Let me say that again: faith, if it is Godly faith, will be validated by faithfulness. Once these more important, faith-proving works are shown, then the offerings will be acceptable and even very pleasing to him.

It was taught in great detail by Jesus, what were the most important matters in the law, as he, in response to the scribe's question says:

> Mar 12:29 Jesus answered, "The most important is, 'Hear, O Israel: Yahweh our God, Yahweh is one.
>
> Mar 12:30 And you shall love Yahweh your God with all your heart and with all your soul and with all your mind and with all your strength.'
>
> Mar 12:31 The second is this: 'You shall love your neighbor as yourself.' There is no other commandment greater than these."

If the foundation of what you do lies in the things Jesus is talking about here, then your motivation is pure. The scribe, understanding that there are things on the opposite end of the law, that can easily be done for reasons outside of faith, responds by saying:

> Mar 12:32 And the scribe said to him, "You are right, Teacher. You have truly said that he is one, and there is no other besides him.

Mar 12:33 And to love him with all the heart and with all the understanding and with all the strength, and to love one's neighbor as oneself, is much more than all whole burnt offerings and sacrifices."

Mar 12:34 And when Jesus saw that he answered wisely, he said to him, "You are not far from the kingdom of God." And after that no one dared to ask him any more questions.

Jesus, in complete agreement with the scribe, congratulates his understanding. However, there were many more cases where Jesus had to rebuke the scribes and Pharisees for their ways. Later on, he comes at them saying:

Mat 23:23 "Woe to you, scribes and Pharisees, hypocrites! For you tithe mint and dill and cumin, and have neglected the weightier matters of the law: justice and mercy and faithfulness. These you ought to have done, without neglecting the others.

Jesus tells them them here not to neglect even the smallest matters of the law, but to do them out of a repentant heart that is truly seeking God's desire, and not to do them for other reasons, adding beforehand in this same speech:

Mat 23:5 They do all their deeds to be seen by others...

And again:

Mat 23:28 So you also outwardly appear righteous to others, but within you are full of hypocrisy and lawlessness.

The reason Jesus emphasizes things such as mercy, justice, love and faith is precisely because of the dead works which were being done in the first century. It would have been to no avail to tell the Jews as the center of his message to please God by keeping the festivals, or doing sacrifices. They were already doing these things. It was the hypocrisy in them that was the source of God's displeasure. Although the minor points of the law were not constantly reiterated in his message, he did in fact, teach explicit obedience to even the smallest command.

Paul was adamant about the believers being zealous for good works. As he also says:

Tit 2:14 who gave himself for us to redeem us from all lawlessness and to purify for himself a people for his own possession who are zealous for good works.

If Paul speaks in positive terms of obedience to the law and of good works, what are the works of the law Paul speaks negatively about? They are those works relating to the law that are done for reasons outside of faith toward God. Paul speaks of Israel in this way:

Rom 9:30 What shall we say, then? That Gentiles who did not pursue righteousness have attained it, that is, a righteousness that is by faith;

Rom 9:31 but that Israel who pursued a law that would lead to righteousness did not succeed in reaching that law.

Rom 9:32 Why? Because they did not pursue it by faith, but as if it were based on works. They have stumbled over the stumbling stone,

Many Jews of that time thought being Jewish was the ticket to get them into the kingdom, so they practiced very publicly those things that identified them as Jewish.

What came to be called the circumcision party insisted that people had to identify themselves as a Jew by converting to Judaism before they could be saved. This included stringent adherence to not only Torah requirements but Rabbinic oral laws as well. Paul and the other apostles taught otherwise. For this reason, the Jerusalem council was convened to give an authoritative voice to what could be considered the entry level requirements for gentiles wishing to adopt this oh so Jewish faith. Having established the basic entry requirements[105] for those who had come to a saving knowledge of the Savior and wishing to fellowship within the Assembly, the believer was expected to then continue in growth by learning Moses in the weekly synagogue meetings.

---

[105] Act 15:19 Wherefore my sentence is, that we trouble not them, which from among the Gentiles are turned to God:
Act 15:20 But that we write unto them, that they abstain from pollutions of idols, and from fornication, and from things strangled, and from blood.
Act 15:21 For Moses of old time hath in every city them that preach him, being read in the synagogues every sabbath day.

Peter tells them plainly that their justification was by faith alone, apart from works related to the law. He tells them how obedience to the whole Torah as a means of justification is a burden neither they nor their forefathers could bear.

In teaching that adding anything to faith as a requirement for salvation, the Pharisees were in fact not operating in faith but were in fact preaching another gospel. Accepting this perverted gospel was a sign they did not believe the sacrifice of God's son was sufficient and thus evidence of a severe lack of faith towards God. For this reason, Paul severely rebukes the Galatians who accept this, as he says to them:

> Gal 3:1 O foolish Galatians, who hath bewitched you, that ye should not obey the truth, before whose eyes Jesus Christ hath been evidently set forth, crucified among you? This only would I learn of you, Received ye the Spirit by the works of the law, or by the hearing of faith? Are ye so foolish? having begun in the Spirit, are ye now made perfect by the flesh? Have ye suffered so many things in vain? if it be yet in vain. He therefore that ministereth to you the Spirit, and worketh miracles among you, doeth he it by the works of the law, or by the hearing of faith? [Remember, works of the law meant trying to be saved by works.] Are you so foolish? Having begun by the Spirit, are you now being perfected by the flesh? Did you suffer so many things in vain--if indeed it was in vain? Does he who supplies the Spirit to you and works miracles among you do so by works of the law, or by hearing with faith--

Like Peter, he says concerning those who rely on the law and not on faith:

> Gal 3:10 For all who rely on works of the law are under a curse; for it is written, "Cursed be everyone who does not abide by all things written in the Book of the Law, and do them."

Most teachers today would have us believe Paul was angry with the Galatians for keeping the laws. That makes little sense considering the bigger picture of Galatians. Bible scholars would have us believe Peter did not live like a Jew (concerning obedience to the law), whereas it is clear that the believers of Jerusalem were zealous for the law.[106]

---

[106] Act 21:20 And when they heard it, they glorified the Lord, and said unto him, Thou seest, brother, how many thousands of Jews there are which

Paul tells Peter he was being hypocritical by disassociating from the believing Gentiles because no man will be justified by works of the law, things related to the Torah done outside of faith. But one cannot rely on works of the law for salvation. The law shows us the sins we have committed and condemns us and simply doing more things related to the Torah is not the solution to that problem.

The faith of the Messiah is.

The Pharisees in general were faithless from the start, and the works of the law they were promoting were nothing more than a continuation of their dead works.

Works of the Law and the Dead Sea Scrolls

The term "Works of the Law" predates Paul and the Christian world by hundreds of years.

Arguably the most important discovery of the last century was the unearthing of what have come to be known as the Dead Sea Scrolls. *"Works of the Law"* is also the term in the Dead Sea Scrolls for a group variously called Judaizers, the Circumcision Party and Ebionites. Here is one quote that clearly points to works of the law as perversion of the Torah.

> *"These are some of the pronouncements concerning the law of God. Specifically, some of pronouncements concerning works of the law that we have determined... and all of them concern defiling mixtures and the purity of the sanctuary ..."*

---

believe; and they are all zealous of the law:
Act 21:21 And they are informed of thee, that thou teachest all the Jews which are among the Gentiles to forsake Moses, saying that they ought not to circumcise their children, neither to walk after the customs.
Act 21:22 What is it therefore? the multitude must needs come together: for they will hear that thou art come.
Act 21:23 Do therefore this that we say to thee: We have four men which have a vow on them;
Act 21:24 Them take, and purify thyself with them, and be at charges with them, that they may shave their heads: and all may know that those things, whereof they were informed concerning thee, are nothing; but that thou thyself also walkest orderly, and keepest the law.

"Works of the Law" specifically referred not to the Torah, but to a collection of Rabbinical traditions that the Essenes believed to be above the Torah. This agrees with what Jesus referred to when He accused the Pharisees of making the commandments of God of no effect by elevating the traditions of men to the level of the Word of God.

This is what Paul is referring to as the Works of the Law in his epistles. This is one of the most misunderstood and misinterpreted subjects in Biblical apologetics. It has done as much as any other text to divide and confuse believers in understanding the artificial law/grace debate. Translators reveal that the Works of the Law is a body of writings extant in the first century, the Miqsat Ma'ase Ha-Torah or MMT, making Paul's use of the phrase much more intelligible to modern Christians. The Essene community stood firmly against this perversion while standing firm in their obedience to the Torah of YHWH.

The MMT is translated in Greek as ergoon nomou, the term used by Paul, which is translated into English as works of the law. In light of the use of the phrase in the Qumran documents, it becomes obvious that Paul was actually talking about a view of the law which the Qumran sect held, a view that was current in non-rabbinical, or may I say Biblical Judaism in the first century. It did not become part of Talmudic tradition and did not become part of what we commonly understand as Judaism today. It then passed away. we can now better Paul to get a feel for what Paul is actually attacking. We see what he is saying is done away with. Torah was not done away with. The works of the law were done away with. Paul repeatedly reiterated that it had nothing to do with salvation or the regulations in the Old Testament. It is concerned with the sacrificial and the ceremonial purification laws and trusting in those for salvation. It confers righteousness by works through a misreading of a text.

Under the Law

The phrase "under the law" is used by Paul in ten verses, listed here:

Rom. 3:19

Rom. 6:14

Rom. 6:15

1 Cor. 9:20

1 Cor. 9:21

Gal. 3:23

Gal. 4:4

Gal. 4:5

Gal. 4:21

Gal. 5:18

The idea that being "under the Law" means having to observe or keep the Torah/Law of Moses is deeply ingrained in much Christian thought. Have you ever considered the view that redeemed people not being "under the Law" might mean something other than what you've been taught? Did you ever consider that "under the Law" might refer to being subject to the Torah's condemnation upon sinners and its consequences and not the the law itself? Did Paul do away with the Commandments of God, that is, establish a new doctrine of grace, one that undeniably brings the Church into lawlessness? OR did the Church allow Marcion, Simon Magus, Constantine, and a host of others to replace God's law with its own traditions, and then use a specious interpretation of Paul's words to justify the move? Christians read Paul's words with a predetermined mindset that is already convinced the law is done away with, rather than view them through the lens of his Jewishness and Torah observance. Ironically, Jewish anti-missionaries do the same thing by using Christian interpretation of Paul's letters to disprove Jesus' claims to Messiahship and the validity of the Apostolic writing. Many in Hebrew Roots circles come to reject Paul for the same reason: they DO NOT interpret Paul correctly in light of his adamant defense of Torah. Could it be that Paul draws a distinction between the law itself and the consequences of breaking that law?

"TORACYSIS"
TORALISISS (JUD's)
↳ LIKE PARALYSIS

What did Paul say about Lawlessness (Torahlessness)?

Here is Romans 6:19 with commentary in brackets: "I speak after the manner of men [in human terms] because of the infirmity of your flesh [the frailty inherent in the natural]: for as ye have yielded your members servants to uncleanness and to iniquity unto iniquity [lawlessness that leads to more lawlessness]; even so now yield your members servants to righteousness [empowered by grace to live rightly according to Torah] unto holiness [being set apart, spirit, soul and body]."

148

According to Titus 2:14, Jesus came to redeem us from **lawlessness**, not from the **law**! *"… who gave himself for us to redeem us from all lawlessness and to purify for himself a people for his own possession who are zealous for good works."*

John the apostle has this to say about lawlessness: 1 John 3:4 *"Whosoever committeth sin transgresseth also the law* [practices lawlessness]: *for sin is the transgression of the law* [going contrary to the law; lawless].

Just as there are physical laws that govern how the universe works, there are spiritual laws. There is the Law of sin and death, death being the Curse of the Law. The natural cause and effect of sin is this. Breaking the law leads to an inevitable consequence, death. The Law is not the curse. The "Curse of the Law' is the result of breaking it.

In Psalm 119 God calls His Law a blessing. If you try to get saved by keeping it, then you fall under a curse because you have already broken it and failed. The law against murder is not a curse. It serves as a deterrent to keep us safe. However, if you murder someone you experience the "Curse of the Law", the death penalty, because you broke that Law.

There is the "The Perfect Law that gives Liberty", the Torah, as G-d states that His Laws give us long life and freedom in Deuteronomy 30.

Paul wrote in Romans 7:12 *"Wherefore the law is holy, and the commandment holy, and just, and good."*

The Law of Sin is the compulsion of a sinner to continue in sin.

Verse 14 says *"For we know that the law is spiritual: but I am carnal, sold under sin."*

Verse 17 *"Now then it is no more I that do it, but sin that dwelleth in me."*

Verses 22, 23 *"For I delight in the law of God after the inward man but I see another law in my members, warring against the law of my mind, and bringing me into captivity to the law of sin which is in my members."*

When one dies to himself, he is released from the law of sin. He is no longer a slave to sin but is now under the perfect law that gives liberty and now a slave to righteousness. We are either slaves to sin or slaves to righteousness. Paul said we must choose. We are never free to just do our own thing. That is called lawlessness. In 2nd Corinthians Paul shows that righteousness and lawlessness are incompatible. *"What fellowship can Light have with Darkness? What fellowship can Christ have with Baal? What fellowship can righteousness have with unrighteousness?"* The word translated as unrighteousness is the Greek word *anomos*, which means – wait for it – without law or lawlessness.

The English word *antinomian* is a theological term in Christian theology that comes from the Greek work *anomos*. It is a term for the teaching that Christians are under no obligation to obey the Old Testament laws of ethics or morality. The many Christians I've talked with vehemently deny being antinomian, or lawless, while at same time insisting they are not subject to the Law, since it was supplanted by a new law called Grace. The irony seems inescapable.

Antinomianism can be seen as diametrically opposed to legalism, the doctrine that teaches obedience to a code of religious law is necessary for salvation. In reality, both antinomianism and legalism are on opposite extremes of the spectrum.

The law was not a set of random rules that God arbitrarily dropped onto his people as they gathered around the foot of the mountain to restrict their freedom. They are an expression of his divine nature. They were given to show former slaves what righteousness in their lives looked like. It is absurd to think God would take His people out of one bondage only to force them into another kind of bondage. The law was not given to restrict his people from freedom. They were given but to release them into it! As James says *"But whoso looketh into the perfect law of liberty, and continueth therein, he being not a forgetful hearer, but a doer of the work, this man shall be blessed in his deed."* James 1:25

Pattern – Principle – Precept

King David wrote, *"Blessed is the man who fears the Lord, who finds great delight in his commands"* Ps. 112:1. I am a man who stands in awe of God's love and grace. I also take great delight in all of his word. I have found that grace doesn't render the law irrelevant to me but actually makes it even more relevant for me. Why? Because the same law that was written on tablets of stone is now written on my heart. Nothing brings greater release out of bondage and into perfect liberty than pleasing the Father by walking out in a practical way what He has written there.

In the law, man was provided the PRECEPT—that is, the divine rule that taught godly behavior. Every precept of God is based upon a PRINCIPLE—that is, the divine reason behind the rule. The principle is based on the PATTERN. God in His perfect holiness is the pattern: *"Be ye holy as I am holy"*. The principle is the desire of God to have a peculiar people who reflect the divine pattern. The law is the precept that defines the steps to lead one to the desired result. All three are manifest fully in the person of Jesus Christ and it is His life in us that grants the faith, ability and the will to be conformed to that image. Under grace we come to understand the principles that drove the precept and see beyond the principle to more fully see the Pattern. Paul was right on when he said, *"the law was our tutor"* (Gal. 3:24). The law is our instruction manual, the blueprint that guides us in our task of building the Temple of God, which is our bodies, or more cogently, the Body of Messiah.

The Pharisees found satisfaction in their strict adherence to all 613 precepts. Outwardly they looked incredibly religious. Jesus said they were whitewashed tombs, filled with dead men's bones. They knew the precepts but couldn't grasp the principles. Jesus was the perfect picture of not just the precepts but the principles as well. Being God in the flesh, He also was the perfect demonstration of the Pattern revealed in Himself. He taught that all the law was based on love. Love for God and love for others. Without love, you'd never understand the law,[107] let alone uphold it.[108]

The Pharisees would criticize Jesus for healing a man on the Sabbath. To them this was work, which dishonored the precept. Their understanding of the law would rather leave a man sick, lame or dead than to see him made whole on a holy day. That's absurd, but then all of man's religion is ludicrous at its core. Jesus told them they didn't understand the principle. *"The Sabbath was made for man, not man for the Sabbath"* Mark 2:27

When we see the principles behind the precepts, we begin to see God's truth, which leads to wisdom. These truths can then be applied to every aspect of life. God's wisdom always produces the greatest blessings. The more I understand and utilize the truth of God, the more I am blessed. Therefore, like David, *"O how love I thy law! it is my meditation all the day. Thou through thy commandments hast made me wiser than mine enemies: for they are ever with me."* Ps. 119:97, 98

---

[107] Mat 22:40 On these two commandments hang all the law and the prophets.
[108] Gal 5:14 For all the law is fulfilled in one word, even in this; Thou shalt love thy neighbour as thyself.

10
THE LORD'S DAY

Jer 16:19 *"O LORD, my strength, and my fortress, and my refuge in the day of affliction, the Gentiles shall come unto thee from the ends of the earth, and shall say, Surely our fathers have inherited lies, vanity, and things wherein there is no profit."*

Considered by many to be a leading Christian apologist, John MacArthur makes the case for the Christian practice of replacing the seventh day with the first day as the set apart day of worship, the Christian Sabbath as some call it. The following quote sums up his analysis of what he deems to be the Biblical reasoning behind the change from the seventh day to the first day.

*"There is no question about the other nine commandments being permanent and binding. We are to have no other gods. We are never to make an idol. We are to worship only the true and living God. We are never to take the name of the Lord in vain. We are not to dishonor our father or mother, but rather give them honor. We are not to murder, commit adultery, steal, lie, or covet. Those are all moral mandates, moral commands, with the exception of verses 8 through 11, the fourth command regarding the sabbath. And the question that is often posed is a simple one. If all the other commands are permanent, is not this one permanent, as well?"; "... when Jesus came, everything changed, everything changed. He didn't just want to clean up the people's attitudes as they gave their sacrifices, He obliterated the sacrificial system because He brought an end to Judaism with all its ceremonies, all its rituals, all its sacrifices, all of its external trappings, the temple, the holy of holies, all of it, **including the sabbath, including the sabbath.***

152

The sabbath observance went away with all the rest that belonged to Judaism." –*Sermon by John MacArthur* [Emphasis mine] - Full sermon can be found on the internet http://www.gty.org/resources/print/sermons/90-379

How is the modern Christian to understand which parts of the Bible are valid and applicable to the believer today and which are to be rejected? Simple. MacArthur affirms nine out of ten commandments he likes and labels anything he doesn't like as "belonging to Judaism". As long as you label any commandment you don't want to follow as *Jewish*, you're on solid ground hermeneutically, at least according to the orthodox Christian method of interpretation. At least MacArthur is honest about his blatant replacement theology. Sounds a lot like the church fathers we quoted in a previous chapter. Nothing ever really advanced from there; just repackaged and regurgitated by countless theologians and Bible commentators.

The question might be asked, how could 2000 years of Church history be wrong about the Sabbath day? Good question. Let's look at a few quotes selected from a long list of references in Church history that speak directly to the Sabbath question in virtually every century beginning with the Lord of the Sabbath himself:

Jesus

 "And he came to Nazareth, where he had been brought up: and, as his custom was, he went into the synagogue on the Sabbath day, and stood up for to read." Luke 4:16

Paul and Gentiles

"And when the Jews were gone out of the synagogue, the Gentiles besought that these words might be preached to them the next Sabbath. And the next Sabbath came almost the whole city together to hear the Word of God." Acts 13:42, 44.

Second Century 100-200

"The primitive Christians had a great veneration for the Sabbath, and spent the day in devotion and sermons. And it is not to be doubted but they derived this practice from the Apostles themselves, as appears by several scriptures to the purpose." -Dialogues on the Lord's Day, p. 189. London: 1701, By Dr. T.H. Morer (A Church of England divine).

"The primitive Christians did keep the Sabbath of the Jews;. . .therefore the Christians, for a long time together, did keep their conventions upon the Sabbath, in which some portions of the law were read: and this continued till the time of the Laodicean council." -The Whole Works of Jeremy Taylor, Vol. IX,p. 416 (R. Heber's Edition, Vol XII, p. 416).

"As early as A.D. 225 there existed large bishoprics or conferences of the Church of the East (Sabbath-keeping) stretching from Palestine to India." Mingana -Early Spread of Christianity. Vol.10, p. 460.

"The seventh-day Sabbath was. . .solemnised by Christ, the Apostles, and primitive Christians, till the Laodicean Council did in manner quite abolish the observations of it." -Dissertation on the Lord's Day," pp. 33, 34

Fourth Century 300-400

"Thou shalt observe the Sabbath, on account of Him who ceased from His work of creation, but ceased not from His work of providence: it is a rest for meditation of the law, not for idleness of the hands." -The Ante-Nicene Fathers," Vol 7,p. 413 from "Constitutions of the Holy Apostles," a document of the 3rd and 4th Centuries.

"It was the practice generally of the Easterne Churches; and some churches of the west...For in the Church of Millaine (Milan);...it seems the Saturday was held in a farre esteeme... Not that the Easterne Churches, or any of the rest which observed that day, were inclined to Iudaisme (Judaism); but that they came together on the Sabbath day, to worship Iesus (Jesus) Christ the Lord of the Sabbath." -History of the Sabbath" [original spelling retained], Part 2, par. 5, pp.73, 74. London: 1636. Dr. Heylyn.

"Ambrose, the celebrated bishop of Milan, said that when he was in Milan he observed Saturday, but when in Rome observed Sunday. This gave rise to the proverb, 'When you are in Rome, do as Rome does.'" Heylyn, "The History of the Sabbath" (1612)

Fifth Century 400-500

"For although almost all churches throughout The World celebrated the sacred mysteries (the Lord's Supper) on the Sabbath of every week, yet the Christians of Alexandria and at Rome, on account of some ancient tradition, refuse to do this." The footnote which accompanies the foregoing quotation explains the use of the word "Sabbath." It says: *"That is, upon the Saturday. It should be observed, that Sunday is never called "the Sabbath' by the ancient Fathers and historians."* Socrates, "Ecclesiastical History," Book 5, chap. 22, p. 289.

"The people of Constantinople, and almost everywhere, assemble together on

154

the Sabbath, as well as on the first day of the week, which custom is never observed at Rome or at Alexandria."-Socrates, "Ecclesiastical History," Book 7, chap.19.

The World – Augustine, Bishop Of Hippo (North Africa)

Augustine shows here that the Sabbath was observed in his day *"in the greater part of the Christian world,"* and his testimony in this respect is all the more valuable because he himself was an earnest and consistent Sunday-keeper. See "Nicene and Post-Nicene Fathers," 1st Series, Vol.1, pp. 353, 354.

Sixth Century 500-600

"In this latter instance they seemed to have followed a custom of which we find traces in the early monastic church of Ireland by which they held Saturday to be the Sabbath on which they rested from all their labours." W.T. Skene, "Adamnan Llife of St. Columbs" 1874, p.96.

"We seem to see here an allusion to the custom, observed in the early monastic Church of Ireland, of keeping the day of rest on Saturday, or the Sabbath." "History of the Catholic Church in Scotland," Vol.1, p. 86, by Catholic histsorian Bellesheim.

Professor James C. Moffatt, D.D., Professor of Church History at Princeton, says: *"It seems to have been customary in the Celtic churches of early times, in Ireland as well as Scotland, to keep Saturday, the Jewish Sabbath, as a day of rest from labour. They obeyed the fourth commandment literally upon the seventh day of week."*-The Church in Scotland, p.140.

"The Celts used a Latin Bible unlike the Vulgate (R.C.) and kept Saturday as a day of rest, with special religious services on Sunday."-Flick, "The Rise of Mediaeval Church," p. 237

Tenth Century 900-1000

"They worked on Sunday, but kept Saturday in a Sabbatical manner."-A history of Scotland from the Roman Occupation, Vol. I, p.96. Andrew Lang

"The Nestorians eat no pork and keep the Sabbath. They believe in neither auricular confession nor purgatory."-Schaff-Herzog, "The New Encyclopaedia of Religious Knowledge," art. "Nestorians."

In reference to the Waldenses: *"And because they observed no other day of rest but the Sabbath days, they called them Insabathas, as much as to say, as they observed no Sabbath."*-Luther's "Fore-Runners" (original spelling), pp. 7, 8

Eleventh Century 1000-1100

"They worked on Sunday, but kept Saturday in a Sabbatical manner." -A history of Scotland from the Roman Occupation, Vol. I, p. 96. Andrew Lang

Sixteenth Century 1500-1600

England: *"In the reign of Elizabeth, it occurred to many conscientious and independent thinkers (as it previously had done to some Protestants in Bohemia) that the fourth commandment required of them the observance, not of the first, but of the specified 'seventh' day of the week."* -Chambers' Cyclopaedia, article "Sabbath," Vol. 8, p. 462, 1537

Sweden: *"This zeal for Saturday-keeping continued for a long time: even little things which might strengthen the practice of keeping Saturday were punished."* -Bishop Anjou, "Svenska Kirkans Historia after Motetthiers, Upsala

Lichenstein Family: (estates in Austria, Bohemia, Morovia, Hungary. Lichenstein in the Rhine Valley wasn't their country until the end of the 7th century). *"The Sabbatarians teach that the outward Sabbath, i.e. Saturday, still must be observed; they say that Sunday is the Pope's invention."* -Refutation of Sabbath, by Wolfgang Capito, published 1599

Bohemia (the Bohemian Brethren): Dr. R. Cox says: *"I find from a passage in Erasmus that at the early period of the Reformantion when he wrote, there were Sabbatarians in Bohemia, who not only kept the seventh day, but were said to be...scrupulous in resting on it."* -Literature of the Sabbath Question, Cox, Vol. II, pp. 201, 202

Historian's List Of Churches (16th Century)
"Sabbatarians, so called because they reject the observance of the Lord's day as not commanded in Scripture, they consider the Sabbath alone to be holy, as God rested on that day and commanded to keep it holy and to rest on it." - A. Ross

Eighteenth Century 1700-1800

"The Jacobites assembled on the Sabbath day, before the Domical day, in the temple, and kept that day, as do also the Abyssinians as we have seen from the confession of their faith by the Ethiopian king Claudius." - Abundacnus, 'Historia Jacobatarum, p.118-9 (18th Century)

Romania, 1760 (and what is today) Yugoslavia, Czechoslovakia

"Joseph II's edict of tolerance did not apply to the Sabbatarians, some of whom again lost all of their possessions." -Jahrgang 2, 254

Twentieth Century 1900-2000

Whoa! Hold on there. How come there's no mention in all the modern Christian literature about the seventh day? Well, here it is.

"The evaluation of Sunday, the traditionally accepted day of the resurrection of Christ, has varied greatly throughout the centuries of the Christian Era. From time to time it has been confused with the seventh day of the week, the Sabbath. English speaking peoples have been the most consistent in perpetuating the erroneous assumption that the obligation of the fourth commandment has passed over to Sunday. In popular speech, Sunday is frequently, but erroneously, spoken of as the Sabbath." -F. M. SETZLER, Head Curator, Department of Anthropology, Smithsonian Institute, from a letter dated Sept. 1, 1949.

"There is nothing in Scripture that requires us to keep Sunday rather than Saturday as a holy day." -Harold Lindsell (editor), Christianity Today, Nov. 5, 1976

Anglican:

"There is no word, no hint, in the New Testament about abstaining from work on Sunday.... Into the rest of Sunday [i.e., Sunday as a day of rest and worship] no divine law enters.... The observance of Ash Wednesday or Lent stands on exactly the same footing as the observance of Sunday." Canon Eyton, The Ten Commandments.

"Where are we told in Scripture that we are to keep the first day at all? We are commanded to keep the seventh; but we are nowhere commanded to keep the first day.... The reason why we keep the first day of the week holy instead of the seventh is for the same reason that we observe many other things, not because the Bible, but because the church has enjoined it." Isaac Williams, D. D., Plain Sermons on the Catechism, vol. 1, pp. 334-336

Episcopal

"The Bible commandment says on the seventh-day thou shalt rest. That is Saturday. Nowhere in the Bible is it laid down that worship should be done on Sunday." Phillip Carrington, quoted in Toronto Daily Star, Oct 26, 1949, Anglican archbishop of Quebec, spoke the above in a message on this subject delivered to a packed assembly of clergymen. It was widely reported at the time in the news media].

Christian: (non-denominational)

"There is no direct scriptural authority for designating the first day the Lord's day." Dr. D. H. Lucas, Christian Oracle, Jan. 23, 1890.

"I do not believe that the Lord's day came in the room [place] of the Jewish Sabbath, or that the Sabbath was changed from the seventh to the first day, for this plain reason, where there is no testimony, there can be no faith. Now there is no testimony in all the oracles that the Sabbath was changed, or that the Lord's day came in the room [place] of it." Alexander Campbell, Washington Reporter, Oct. 8, 1821.[Ed. note: Then why does he persist in calling Sunday the Lord's day?]

Church of Christ

"I do not believe that the Lord's day came in the room (place) of the Jewish Sabbath, or that the Sabbath was changed from the seventh to the first day, for this plain reason, where there is no testimony, there can be no faith. Now there is no testimony in all the Oracles that the Sabbath was changed, or that the Lord's day came in the room (place) of it." Quote from the founder of the Church of Christ, Alexander Campbell, in the Washington Reporter, Oct. 8, 1821.

"There is no direct scriptural authority for designating the first day the Lord's day." Dr. D. H. Lucas, Christian Oracle, Jan. 23, 1890.

"The seventh day was observed from Abraham's time, nay, from creation. The Jews identified their own history with the institution of the Sabbath day. They loved and venerated it as a patriarchal usage." "The evidence of Christianity" Page 302 Saint Louis: Christian Publishing co. 1906, Quoted from a debate between Robert Owen and Alexander Campbell (The founder of the Church of Christ), Saint Louis: Christian Publishing co. 1906.

"But we do not find any direct command from God, or instruction from the risen Christ, or admonition from the early apostles, that the first day is to be substituted for the seventh day Sabbath." "Let us be clear on this point. Though to the Christian 'that day, the first day of the week' is the most memorable of all days ... there is no command or warrant in the New Testament for observing it as a holy day." "The Roman Church selected the first day of the week in honour of the resurrection of Christ. ..." Bible Standard, May, 1916, Auckland, New Zealand.

Congregationalist:

"It must be confessed that there is no law in the New Testament concerning the first day [Sunday]." -Buck's Theological Dictionary.

"The current notion that Christ and His apostles authoritatively substituted the first day for the seventh, is absolutely without authority in the New Testament." -Dr. Lyman Abbott, Christian Union, Jan. 19, 1882.

"It is clear that, however rigidly or devoutly we may spend Sunday, we are not keeping the Sabbath ... The Sabbath was founded on a specific divine command. We can plead no such command for the obligation to observe Sunday ... There is not a single sentence in the New Testament to suggest that we incur any penalty by violating the supposed sanctity of Sunday." -Dr. Dale, The Ten Commandments, pp. 106, 107.

Lutheran:

"We have seen how gradually the impression of the Jewish Sabbath faded from the mind of the Christian church, and how completely the newer thought underlying the observance of the first day took possesion of the church. We have seen that the Christian of the first three centuries never confused one with the other, but for a time celebrated both." -The Sunday Problem, a study book by the Lutheran Church (1923) p.36

"I wonder exceedingly how it came to be imputed to me that I should reject the law of Ten Commandments.... Whosoever abrogates the law must of necessity, abrogate sin also." -Martin Luther, Spiritual Antichrist, pp. 71,72.

"They [the Catholics] allege the Sabbath changed into Sunday, the Lord's day, contrary to the decalogue, as it appears, neither is there any example more boasted of than the changing of the Sabbath day. Great, they say, is the power and authority of the church, since it dispensed with one of the Ten Commandments." -Authored by Philipp Melanchthon with approval by Martin Luther, Augsburg Confession of Faith, Art. 28, Par. 9.

But they err in teaching that Sunday has taken the place of the Old Testament Sabbath and therefore must be kept as the seventh day had to be kept by the children of Israel. In other words, they insist that Sunday is the divinely appointed New Testament Sabbath, and so they endeavor to enforce the Sabbatical observance of Sunday by so-called blue laws.... These churches err in their teaching, for Scripture has in no way ordained the first day of the week in place of the Sabbath. There is simply no law in the New Testament to that effect." -John T. Mueller, Sabbath or Sunday?, pp. 15,16.

"The observance of the Lord's Day (Sunday) is founded not on any command of God, but on the authority of the Church." -Augsburg Confession of Faith.

Methodist:

"This 'handwriting of ordinances' *our Lord did blot out, take away, and nail to His cross. (Colossians 2:14.) But the moral law contained in the ten commandments, and enforced by the prophets, He did not take away the moral law, [the Ten Commandments], stands on an entirely different foundation from the ceremonial or ritual law.... Every part of this law must remain in force upon all mankind and in all ages."* -John Wesley, Sermons on Several Occasions, 2 vol. ed., vol. 1, pp. 221, 222.

"It is true that there is no positive command for infant baptism. Nor is there any for keeping holy the first day of the week. Many believe that Christ changed the Sabbath. But, from his own words, we see that he came for no such purpose. Those who believe that Jesus changed the Sabbath base it ONLY on a SUPPOSITION." -Amos Binney, "Theological Compendium" pp. 180-181.

Presbyterian:

"The Sabbath is part of the Decalogue - the Ten Commandments. This alone forever settles the question as to the perpetuity of the institution.... Until therefore it can be shown that the whole moral law has been repealed, the Sabbath will stand.... The teaching of Christ confirms the perpetuity of the Sabbath." -T. C. Blake, D. D., Theology Condensed, pp. 474, 475.

"We must not imagine that the coming of Christ has freed us from the authority of the law; for it is the eternal rule of a devout and holy life, and must therefore be as unchangeable as the justice of God, which if embraced, is constant and uniform." -John Calvin, Commentary on a Harmony of the Gospels, vol. 1, p. 277.

"The Christian Sabbath [Sunday] is not in the Scriptures, and was not by the primitive church called the Sabbath." -Dwight's Theology, Vol. 14, p. 401.

"A further argument for the perpetuity of the Sabbath we have in Matthew 24:20, Pray ye that your flight be not in the winter neither on the Sabbath day. But the final destruction of Jerusalem was after the Christian dispensation was fully set up (AD 70). Yet it is plainly implied in these words of the Lord that even then Christians were bound to strict observation of the Sabbath." -Works of Jonathan Edwards, (Presby.) Vol. 4, p. 621.

Moody Bible Institute:

"The Sabbath was binding in Eden, and it has been in force ever since. The

fourth commandment begins with the word 'remember,' showing that the Sabbath already existed when God wrote the law on the tables of stone at Sinai. How can men claim that this one commandment has been done away when they will admit that the other nine are still binding?" -Dwight L. Moody, Weighed and Wanting, p. 47

"I honestly believe that this commandment is just as binding to-day as it ever was. I have talked with men who have said that it has been abrogated, but they have never been able to point to any place in the Bible where God repealed it."When Christ was on earth He did nothing to set it [the Sabbath] aside; He freed it from the traces under which the scribes and Pharisees had put it, and gave it its true place.'The Sabbath was made for man, and not man for the Sabbath.' It is just as practicable and as necessary for men today as it ever was - in fact, more than ever, because we live in such an intense age." -Dwight L. Moody, Weighed and Wanting

"There has been an awful letting-down in this country regarding the sabbath during the last twenty-five years, and many a man has been shorn of spiritual power, like Samson, because he is not straight on this question. Can you say that you observe the sabbath properly? You may be a professed Christian: are you obeying this commandment? Or do you neglect the house of God on the sabbath day ...?" -[ibid]

The sabbath was binding in Eden, and it has been in force ever since. This fourth commandment begins with the word "remember," showing that the sabbath already existed when God wrote this law on the tables of stone at Sinai. How can men claim that this one commandment has been done away with when they will admit that the other nine are still binding? -[ibid]

I believe that the sabbath question to-day is a vital one for the whole country. It is the burning question of the present time. If you give up the sabbath the church goes; if you give up the church the home goes; and if the home goes the nation goes. That is the direction in which we are traveling. -[ibid] [ed. Note: the world and particularly the US, has been in an accelerating downward spiral into moral decay since Moody wrote these words.]

Baptist:

"We believe that the law of God is the eternal and imperishable rule of His moral government." Baptist Church Manual.

"The first four commandments set forth man's obligations directly toward God.... The fourth commandment sets forth God's claim on man's time and thought.... Not one of the ten words [commandments] is of merely racial significance.... The Sabbath was established originally [long before Moses] in no special connection with the Hebrews, but as an institution for all mankind, in commemoration of God's rest after six days of creation. It was designed for all the descendants of Adam." -Adult Quarterly, Southern Baptist Convention series, Aug. 15, 1937.

"There was and is a commandment to keep holy the Sabbath day, but that Sabbath day was not Sunday. .... It will be said, however, and with some show of triumph, that the Sabbath was transferred from the seventh to the first day of the week. ... Where can the record of such a transaction be found? Not in the New Testament -- absolutely not. There is no scriptural evidence of the change of the Sabbath institution from the seventh to the first day of the week.

"To me [it] seems unaccountable that Jesus, during three years' intercourse with His disciples, often conversing with them. upon the Sabbath question ... never alluded to any transference of the day; also that during forty days of His resurrection life, no such thing was intimated.

"Of course, I quite well know that Sunday did come into use in early Christian history as a religious day, as we learn from the Christian Fathers and other sources. But what a pity that it comes branded with the mark of paganism, and christened with the name of the sun god, when adopted and sanctioned by the papal apostasy, and bequeathed as a sacred legacy to Protestantism!" -Dr. Edward T. Hiscox, author of The Baptist Manual (still in print), in a paper read before New York ministers' conference held Nov.13, 1893.

How the Seventh Day Became the First Day and Other Confusing Arithmetic

If Jesus didn't change the seventh day to the first day; if the Apostles and early disciples didn't change the day to Sunday; if the Church historically kept the seventh day Sabbath; if the major denominational leadership admits there is no Scriptural basis for making the change, WHO CHANGED IT!

The answer is probably already pretty well understood, even if you've never given conscious consideration to the question. But let's hear it from the Mother Church herself:

"It is well to remind the Presbyterians, Baptists, Methodists, and all other Christians, that the Bible does not support them anywhere in their observance

of Sunday. Sunday is an institution of the Roman Catholic Church, and those who observe the day observe a commandment of the Catholic Church." - Priest Brady, in an address, reported in the Elizabeth, NJ 'News' on March 18, 1903. See This Rock

"Most Christians assume that Sunday is the biblically approved day of worship. The Roman Catholic Church protests that it transferred Christian worship from the biblical Sabbath (Saturday) to Sunday, and that to try to argue that the change was made in the Bible is both dishonest and a denial of Catholic authority. If Protestantism wants to base its teachings only on the Bible, it should worship on Saturday." -Mary Online

"Deny the authority of the Church and you have no adequate or reasonable explanation or justification for the substitution of Sunday for Saturday in the Third – Protestant Fourth – Commandment of God… The Church is above the Bible, and this transference of Sabbath observance is proof of that fact." -Catholic Record, September 1, 1923.

"If Protestants would follow the Bible, they would worship God on the Sabbath Day. In keeping the Sunday they are following a law of the Catholic Church." -Albert Smith, Chancellor of the Archdiocese of Baltimore, replying for the Cardinal, in a letter dated February 10, 1920.

"Protestants … accept Sunday rather than Saturday as the day for public worship after the Catholic Church made the change… But the Protestant mind does not seem to realize that … in observing Sunday, they are accepting the authority of the spokesman for the Church, the pope." -Our Sunday Visitor, February 5th, 1950. See This Rock

"The Church, on the other hand, after changing the day of rest from the Jewish Sabbath, or seventh day of the week, to the first, made the Third Commandment refer to Sunday as the day to be kept holy as the Lord's Day. The Council of Trent (Sess. VI, can. xix) condemns those who deny that the Ten Commandments are binding on Christians." -The Catholic Encyclopedia, Commandments of God, Volume IV, © 1908 by Robert Appleton Company – Online Edition © 1999 by Kevin Knight, Nihil Obstat – Remy Lafort, Censor Imprimatur – +John M. Farley, Archbishop of New York, page 153.

"Of course these two old quotations are exactly correct. The Catholic Church designated Sunday as the day for corporate worship and gets full credit – or blame – for the change." -This Rock, The Magazine of Catholic Apologetics and Evangelization, p.8, June 1997

Question: Which is the Sabbath day?
Answer: Saturday is the Sabbath day.

Question: Why do we observe Sunday instead of Saturday?
Answer: We observe Sunday instead of Saturday because the
Catholic Church transferred the solemnity from Saturday to
Sunday."
-Rev. Peter Geiermann C.SS.R., The Convert's Catechism of
Catholic Doctrine, p. 50

Q. Must not a sensible Protestant doubt seriously, when he finds
that even the Bible is not followed as a rule by his co-religionists?
A. Surely, when he sees them baptize infants, abrogate the Jewish
Sabbath, and observe Sunday for which [pg. 7] there is no
Scriptural authority; when he finds them neglect to wash one
another's feet, which is expressly commanded, and eat blood and
things strangled, which are expressly prohibited in Scripture. He
must doubt, if he think at all. …
Q. Should not the Protestant doubt when he finds that he himself
holds tradition as a guide?
A. Yes, if he would but reflect that he has nothing but Catholic
Tradition for keeping the Sunday holy; … Controversial
Catechism by Stephen Keenan, New Edition, revised by Rev.
George Cormack, published in London by Burns & Oates,
Limited – New York, Cincinnati, Chicago: Benzinger Brothers,
1896, pages 6, 7.

After all this evidence pointing to pockets of believers keeping the seventh
day Sabbath, many may still convince themselves that the majority of
Christians kept Sunday holy, and that these quotes only refer to a minority
of believers throughout history who kept the Sabbath, to which I offer a
hearty amen. God has always kept a remnant in every generation.

11
RESTORATION

We come full circle with this final chapter, back to the question of discipleship. The challenge before us now is, will we, the Body of Messiah, follow in the footsteps of Jesus, do as he did, think as he thought, speak as he spoke, worship as he worshiped? Will we walk as He walked[109] or will we discard His clear example and follow the Roman Church as our Church Fathers taught? Choose wisely.

The road to glory is a process. We all begin at the foot of the cross. It is there that confession is made and our hearts believe and receive the promise of eternal life. With hope-filled expectancy, we fix our eyes on the prize and know with certainty that we, like orphans out of place, will one day go home. With starts and stops, victories and failures, we stumble down the path to soon realize the proverbial rubber, when it crashes onto the road before our eyes, exposes a hazard-laden way filled with peril and continual distractions. We learn it is one thing to stand before Calvary's cross and believe. It is quite another to take up that cross and make it a standard that guides our every life decision.

This chapter may well be a turning point in many Christians' lives. Your life may be turned upside down (again). Once a disciple takes up the cross and begins to truly follow in the dust of our Rabbi, one can expect to be rejected, rebuked, turned on by those they trust and love the most. One may be called self-righteous, a legalist, holier than thou, or a host of other

---

[109] 1Jn 2:6 He that saith he abideth in him ought himself also so to walk, even as he walked.

callous invectives. Those who truly love you may attempt to lead you back to a static faith, immobile and unchanging, content to just persevere and wait for the Rapture to take us all out of here. Some well-meaning friends may even mistake the deep conviction and resultant disgust with self you are sure to experience and chalk it off as a momentary lapse of emotional strength. Some may try to soothe it away. Friends, once your soul has tasted the sweetness of God's law, freed from the burden of trying to earn salvation through it, there is no going back. Rather, it is the most profound of all "going backs"; back to our first love, who lived, breathed, walked, talked and demonstrated His Father's law.

Take heart, friends. We are in good company. Our spiritual forebears suffered for the word of their testimony. The unvarnished truth of Scripture is that the righteous will suffer tribulation. There may be a direct correlation between the degree of persecution we suffer and the brightness of the light that shines within and through us. The brighter the light, the clearer the target. It is clear from Revelation 13[110] that Satan's number one target here at the end of this age will be those who keep the Commandments of God AND also have a testimony of Jesus Christ.

A preponderance of scholarly and theological debate within the Church for centuries has been over whether the law is relevant and applicable to the post crucifixion believer or not. Was the law eternal and unchanging or was it only applicable for a season until a more favorable law called grace supplanted it? I refer again to the words of Satan *"Hath God said?"* Careful study of the New Testament reveals the earliest Christians didn't quarrel over **whether** to keep the laws or not, misinterpreted Pauline texts notwithstanding. Their debate centered around **how** to keep the laws.

Angst is a necessary component of spiritual growth. I submit that if faith doesn't stir passion within a person, it is unlikely to produce any change. Growth in the natural as well as in the spiritual will be accompanied by growth pains. Change is not comfortable. Faith, mountain moving, gates of hell assaulting faith, is forged in the fires of testing. If we cannot agonize over the depth of uncleanness in our fallen nature, we'll never truly hate the brokenness inherent in the old nature that still guides our lives. Conviction hurts. But with the proper response, it leads to deep repentance, which in turn leads to an Isaiah experience: *"I am a man of unclean lips ... "*[111] followed

---

[110] Rev 12:17 And the dragon was wroth with the woman, and went to make war with the remnant of her seed, which keep the commandments of God, and have the testimony of Jesus Christ.

[111] Rev 12:17 And the dragon was wroth with the woman, and went to make

by *"... here am I. Send me."*

Being separated from the world is more than getting off drugs or alcohol, of cleaning up a potty mouth or changing other negative habits, although true repentance does have those desired results. On a deeper level, it is a painful separation of our innermost selves from who we were to who we are called to be.

Historically, Catholic priests aided by soldiers forced Christians to accept Papal dictates, compelling them to work on the Sabbath and to attend church on Sunday. Refusal to bow to the decrees of the Roman church led to the most inhumane tortures ever devised in the dark heart of man. Some were beheaded, others burned at the stake, all for simply trying to follow in the path of Jesus. Judging by the evidence of what seems to be a mass return of Protestant Christianity to the mother Catholic Church, those days may well come again.

Where will you stand when the time comes?

If you've stayed with us this far, you will have read what the Church Fathers said. You read what the Catholic Church said. You read what the Fundamental Evangelical Church said. You read what Paul said. For all our sakes, let's see what God said.

Restoration of All Things

The great promise of prophetic Scripture is there will be a restoration of all things[112] to a state of perfection as it was in the beginning. The antithetical dare, the lie of all lies, the all-time greatest, most deceptive ruse of all time, the bewitchment of mankind, is the lie predicated on the satanic challenge *"hath God said"* – **Hath God said?** A simple question. As long as one can question what God actually says, then the sky's the limit for interpreting what He said. Did God really say? Did God really mean not to eat of the fruit? Did He really mean to remember the Sabbath day to keep it holy? Did He really mean for us to distinguish between clean and unclean animals in our dietary menus? Where in all of God's Word is there any indication

---

war with the remnant of her seed, which keep the commandments of God, and have the testimony of Jesus Christ.
[112] Act 3:21 Whom the heaven must receive until the times of restitution of all things, which God hath spoken by the mouth of all his holy prophets since the world began.

whatsoever that man has authority to change one word of what He has revealed? You know the answer.

The Church of God stands on the threshold of an event foretold for millennia, the final campaign of the cosmic war that began with insurrection in the courts of Heaven. At the crossroad of decision, the Church will either maintain the status quo with a Gospel stripped of the Holiness of God's Law, or we in unison will begin to walk as Jesus walked, declaring with our lives the vital union of His matchless Grace and His Immutable Law.

Truth needs no defense. It stands on its own even if no one stands with it. It needs no laws to enforce it. Truth never changes but it will change any who stand in its light. To loosely paraphrase Shakespeare, truth is still true whether in a fool's or a liar's pocket. If the views presented in this book are true, then those opposing them may find themselves in the unenviable position of fighting against the very purposes of the God they claim to believe.[113]

Revival or Restoration?

Winds of change are blowing around the globe in a dizzying move of God in these last days. While evangelistic crusades, revival meetings and renewal conferences have been a mainstay of contemporary Church ministry programs, what is happening today appears to be something very different. Like the mist rising from the earth to water the garden in Eden, the Spirit seems to be moving in a non-localized way to stir hearts with a sense of un-satisfaction and a longing for deeper relationship with the Father; an unsettling sense that something is missing in their everyday church experience. People are experiencing personal revival in Church pews, in Synagogues, in Mosques and everywhere in between.

Multitudes of previously un-reached are coming to know Jesus as Lord and Savior. Muslims in various Islamic countries are experiencing visions and dreams, coming to salvation in unprecedented numbers. Oftentimes, their faith is met with the ultimate test of obedience at the hands of their former

---

[113] Act 5:39 But if it be of God, ye cannot overthrow it; lest haply ye be found even to fight against God.

brothers in Islam.

Jews from all walks of life are coming in increasing numbers to recognize and accept their Jewish Messiah, Yeshua. Professionals, educators, Rabbis, and a host of everyday Jews are leading the way to what may be the beginning stages of the fulfillment of Zech. 12:10.

Ministries are springing up in the land of Israel boldly proclaiming Yeshua the Messiah, reaching millions of Jews and Gentiles around the globe with the Gospel from a Jewish perspective.

Ministries like Rabbi Ariel Cohen Alloro's Facing Each Other Initiative, a project whose stated purpose is seen in this headline on his ministry page The Jewish Initiative for the Legal Return of Yeshua to Israel. In the same document, he writes *"After 2000 years of ideological misunderstandings and misconceptions between Judaism and Christianity, The Facing-Each-Other initiative is undertaking an historical, major, crucial task to reach aut(h)entic reconciliation betwee(n) the 2 main streams of faith that have both emerged from the same Torah received on Mount Sinai."*

Or consider the ministry One for Israel, an outreach that includes a Bible College, Jewish evangelism, humanitarian aid, regularly confronting counter-missionaries with the errors of orthodox Judaism, reaching thousands with the clear message of salvation in Yeshua and Him alone.

Rabbi Yitsak Shapira. Teaching and preaching in revivals in Jewish communities around the world leading many to faith in Messiah while maintaining their Jewish identity and connection to Torah.

The Hebrew Roots Movement, in this writer's opinion, has served its greater purpose of opening the gate to an awareness of the incontrovertible fact of the Church's Jewish roots. Like all movements that preceded it however, it began to crumble under its own weight of superiority and divisive insistence on conformity to various doctrinal creeds. Forsaking attempts at labeling, we submit all that has gone on to this point is simply preparatory to a legitimate return to the ancient path describe by the prophet Jeremiah,[114] a return to our true Biblical Roots.

---

[114] Jer 6:16 Thus saith the LORD, Stand ye in the ways, and see, and ask for the old paths, where is the good way, and walk therein, and ye shall find rest for

Professor Daniel I. Block, Professor of Old Testament a Wheaton College, is a pioneer in bringing the Biblical connection of Christianity to its Hebrew roots to the forefront of mainstream academia. With a long list of accomplishments in Semitic theological study and archaeology, he brings a much-needed voice of scholarly reason to the discussion.

In an essay entitled Preaching Old Testament Law to New Testament Christians, part of a larger work in his book The Gospel According to Moses: Theological and Ethical Reflections on the Book of Deuteronomy.[115] The essay begins with *"I am keenly aware that in proposing [that the Torah of Moses is valid for Christians] I have guaranteed for myself a limited hearing."*

In his review of Block's book, Eugene Merrill of Dallas Theological Seminary says this:

> *"Block is at his very best as a devout Old Testament pastor-teacher in his essay on preaching the Old Testament in the New Testament church. He is right on target with his feeling of despair about the neglect of the Old Testament as relevant and timely Christian Scripture. The* **Marcionite** [emphasis mine] *view of an Old Testament God who is not the God of the New Testament coupled with extreme Lutheranism's dichotomy between law and grace has infected the pulpit to the point of virtually de-canonizing the Old Testament. Block provides in this chapter biblically and theologically sound ways of integrating the Old Testament into the mainstream of evangelical thought and performance without drifting into legalism on the one hand or antinomianism on the other."* Eugene H. Merrill, Dallas Theological Seminary, January 1, 2014

Merrill goes on to say:

> *"The essay on worship In Spirit and in Truth[116] should be mandatory reading in all seminaries in America. With great sensitivity, passion, spiritual depth, and keen exegetical and theological insight Block deftly walks*

---

your souls. But they said, We will not walk therein.

[115]

http://www.amazon.com/gp/product/1610978633?*Version*=1&*entries*=0

[116] ibid

*the tightrope between the importation of Mosaic temple liturgy and ritual into Christian worship and **the unstructured** 'feel good' **narcissism of the modern evangelical church**. Thus he parts company with scholars such as D. A. Carson and John Piper who, in his view, are guilty on two counts: (1) They "underestimate the liturgical nature of worship in the New Testament," and (2) "they misrepresent the shape of true worship as it is presented in the Old Testament" (pp. 274–75). His conclusion is that* **'the time has come for a new generation of biblical scholars, theologians, and pastors to begin focusing on the continuities between Old and New; Israel's faith and Christian faith; and most significantly YHWH the God of Israel, and Jesus Christ, the Lord of the church'"** *(p. 298).* [Emphasis his]

In the essay, Professor Block says misconceptions about the law arise from fundamental ideological and theological prejudices against Old Testament law that can be traced back to a 2nd century heretic by the name of Marcion. Very little effort in a library will yield a mountain of information about this man. Among many other blatant heresies, he taught that there was a radical discontinuity between the Old and New Testaments, in essence setting the foundation for the artificial dam referenced in an earlier chapter. On that foundation, he emphasized a clear division between Israel and the Church, with a radical distinction between the God of the Old Testament and the God of the New.

Block then goes on to identify three current streams of prejudice:

1. The antipathy resulting from the Lutherian law-gospel contrast, [ed. note- another of Marcion's forced distinctions.]
2. The dispensational idea that the church age with its dispensation of grace is fundamentally different *from* the Israel age with its dispensation of law.
3. The New Covenant Theology rooted in Reformed Theology which says that Mosaic Covenant ended when Christ instituted the New Covenant.

Because of these misconceptions, he says most preachers teach that the Law is irrelevant for three reasons:

1. The atoning work of Jesus Christ liberated us from the "curse of the law"
2. The word telos in Rom 10:4 is taken to mean "termination" of the law
3. Christians pick and choose the laws they feel they should keep by differentiating between ceremonial, civil, and moral laws.

Block addresses the misconceptions by exploring the nature of the Law in its literary and cultural context, and how the Law was perceived by Old Testament believers. How did the Old Testament Saints in Israel understand and respond to the Law? His answers dispel the popular notion that the Law was antithetical to Grace, beautifully restoring the vital relationship between the two:

1. They perceived obedience to the laws, not as a precondition to salvation but rather as the grateful response of those who had already been saved
2. They perceived obedience to the law as an expression of covenant relationship—obey the voice of God
3. They perceived obedience to the law as a precondition to achieving the mission to which they'd been called and the precondition to receiving blessing
4. Being able to hear what the God of Israel wanted was considered a unique privilege compared to the gods of the nations who didn't speak. They were thankful to know with clarity and confidence what God wanted for their lives
5. They perceived true obedience to the law to be the external expression of an inward disposition of fear and faith in God and love for God
6. They perceived the laws holistically, viewing all of life as under the authority of the divine suzerain. Whereas many Christians think of the Torah as divisible according to moral, civil, and ceremonial, this classification fails to appreciate the nature and organization of the laws themselves. Thus, they never questioned "which" laws to keep but rather "how" to keep the laws
7. While they believed the commandments were achievable, it was also understood that God, recognizing their propensity to

sin, had provided a means for forgiveness and communion through the sacrificial and ceremonial ritual

Block then characterizes the connection of the Church with Israel. *"There was no time in Israel's history when every Israelite was truly devoted to [Adonai] in this sense. For this reason, within the new Israelite covenant, Jeremiah anticipates a time when the boundaries between physical Israel and spiritual Israel will be coterminous and all will love God and demonstrate with their lives that his [Torah] has been written on their hearts (Jer. 31:31-34)."*

He finds these interpretive traditions remarkable considering the fact that Jesus declared the Law to be unchanging and unchangeable in Matthew 5:17-20, and given His declaration that love for Him is demonstrated first and foremost by keeping His commands (John 14:15; 15:10). The Apostle Paul also asserts that it's the doers of the law who will be justified (Rom. 2:13). [ed. note: not that the law justifies, but that the doers of the law give evidence of an internal change.]

He also questions how Christians can read *"All Scripture is breathed out by God and profitable for teaching, for reproof, for correction, and for training in righteousness, that the person of God may be competent, equipped for every good work"* (2 Tim 3:16-17) as an assertion that Mosaic law is not a requirement but rather as an "optional sourcebook for optional lessons."

Block concludes his essay by adding *"the problem of applying Old Testament laws to contemporary contexts is much more complex than these few summary statements would imply"*, reassuring his readers that he is not advocating any kind of works salvation. Rather, salvation should result in a life that conforms to the will of God.

Salvation by Grace – Gratitude by Works

Once a Christian accepts that obedience to the law is not a repudiation of grace but actually the grateful response of one who desires to walk in submission to the will of God, the meaning of Jesus's words[117] becomes crystal clear. Acknowledging that the law is not a collection of impossible to keep laws from a harsh God from long ago - the God of the Old Testament - but rather instructions for how to live life in the way that pleases God, the only question for the Christian becomes the same one the first century believers asked: not **should** I keep the Law but rather **how** do I apply Old Testament law to my own life?

I am not surprised that a scholar of this distinction is taking a stand for the Law. It is clear to me that we are on the threshold of a major paradigm shift; one that completes the work begun with the Reformation in calling the Church to separation from Mystery Babylon. It will radically divide Christendom into those who walk as the Messiah walked and those who follow after the false messiah, the Lawless One, when he steps onto the world stage. There is a clear division taking shape as the true nature of the wheat and tares is exposed under the revealing light of God's prophetic word. The Church is indeed standing at the crossroad of decision. The direction we take going forward will declare to the world whether we are truly disciples of the Christ of Heaven or are committed to holding onto the lies inherited from our fathers. The great Dragon of Revelation has a singular target: those who have a testimony of Jesus **and** who keep His Commandments. The question before us today is, am I a target? If not, why not?

The End ...

---

[117] Joh 14:15 If ye love me, keep my commandments.

… is just the beginning.

Beloved, the race isn't to the swiftest. It isn't even to the smartest. The race is to those that finish the race. The race is to those who follow the Leader.

I wish you enough sun to keep your attitude bright.
I wish you enough rain to appreciate the sun more.
I wish you enough happiness to keep your spirit alive.
I wish you enough pain so that the smallest joys in life appear much bigger.
I wish you enough gain to satisfy your wanting.
I wish you enough loss to appreciate all that you possess.
I wish you enough "Hellos" to get you through the final "Good-bye." (Author unknown)

My friends, more than anything, I wish you Yeshua.

ABOUT THE AUTHOR

Preston McNutt, Husband, Father, Grandfather, Pastor and Teacher. Forty + years walking with the King of Glory and the longer I walk, the more deeply my soul recognizes its desperate need to crucify the flesh and for Him to cover me with the light of His Glory. One day, like an orphan out of place, I will go home.

44087618R00104

Made in the USA
San Bernardino, CA
06 January 2017